Creations Story

Historical

Scientific

Biblical

PAUL EKROTH

ISBN 978-1-64258-646-6 (paperback)
ISBN 978-1-64258-966-5 (hardcover)
ISBN 978-1-64258-647-3 (digital)

Christian Faith Publishing, Inc.
832 Park Avenue
Meadville, PA 16335
www.christianfaithpublishing.com

Printed in the United States of America

A challenge to science and the religious world. If the first chapter of the Bible is proven to be false, what follows it is also suspect.

In Appreciation

Outside of my own family, no one
has demonstrated more kindness
or willingness to help, other
than Alan and Mary Buckley.

My daughters, Brenda Brown
and Shirley Burkhart, are
the love of my life.

Brenda is not only my secretary
but also my business consultant.

Shirley who lives a distance of
fifteen hundred miles away radiates
love and a willingness to serve
those who she encounters.

Contents

The hidden path reveals the only path that leads
to heaven for both the Jew and the gentile.
The path is concealed and not easily located.
Multitudes follow strange voices. The easy paths
are numerous.
The revelation of the path is made obvious to all
who desire eternal life.

The revelation of our world today and how the
earth will end.
The beast whose number is 666.
What will happen to Israel?
When will the rapture occur?
A glimpse of the new heaven and the new earth.

Introduction

No two scholars are able to agree as to the interpretation of each Bible verse or subject. Thousands of Christian denominations exist, divided by truth as they believe truth to be.

A major dispute divided the early church as to what constituted a true conversion. Those involved included Apostle Paul, Barnabas, Peter, James, Simeon, Silas, and others who in hot dispute departed, unable to agree. Acts 15 Paul, at a later date, wrote, "We know in part, we prophesy in part. But when the perfect comes, the partial will be done away—Now we see in a mirror dimly, but then face to face; now I know in part, but then I shall know fully, just as I also have been fully known" (1 Cor. 13:9–12).

The failure to properly interpret the first chapters of Genesis has caused rejection of the entire Bible by many. If the first chapters of a book are proven to be false, the entire book remains suspect. For thousands of years, there has been no reason to question the authorities who quoted from God that He created the entire universe in six days, and this was completed six thousand years ago. What appeared as sound logic many years ago no longer applies. Truth has not changed. Our understanding of the universe and the Bible has changed. We, at times, find it difficult to admit ignorance in our ability to balance reality with scripture.

The beginning has no date. It is a statement of fact. When the beginning started, it is not stated nor implied. The Bible infers that a civilization had existed on earth prior to Adam. Job, a wealthy man, questioned whether God had the ability to know or to properly rule the universe. Job's answer came in the form of questions. "Job, where were you when I formed the earth? Was it you who decided how large it would be or what type of pillars would be used to support the earth? Who decided that there would be a night and day? Tell Me, if you are able." God then named and described creatures that at one time existed on earth. They were made of flesh, as was Job, but Job knew nothing of their existence (Book of Job).

The Bible is unlike any other books. Other books considered sacred by their followers such as the Koran, Book of Mormon, Science and Health, The Zend Avesta, Classics of Confucius were written by humans. We know when they were born, and we know when they died.

Biblical history began before the earth's existence. When God first created the heavens. Long before there was an Adam and long before there was an Eve, the Bible provides a description of creatures that once roamed on the earth.

The Bible consists of a collection of sixty-six books that were written by forty-four individuals throughout twenty centuries of time. Some of these spokespersons represented entire nations as was King David and King Solomon.

Their central theme was not based on their own popularity, rather on the greatness of God who created the heavens and the earth. Each human story exposed scandals as well as the good things that were done. It tells how God became a friend to the very poor and as well to the very rich. This is the story of sixty-six-plus people who met God in the quietness of their own lives. Most are strangers to each other. Time, language, and location gaps separated the stories beyond four thousand years.

Each story is unique. Each story reveals God from a different perspective. The Bible is God's revelation of Himself and He invites all to His table of knowledge.

Chapter 1

The Heavens

Heaven and the firmament are one and the same (Gen. 1:8). The firmament is the heaven that engulfs the earth. The size of the universe is determined by the creator.

From Adam to the nineteenth century, humanity has believed that the Milky Way galaxy was the extent of the universe. Discoveries in the past two hundred years have uncovered a universe that startles one's imagination and has caused excitement to the world of astronomy. True, the Milky Way galaxy contains over a billion stars. Looking beyond the Milky Way, the heavens are filled with tiny specks of light. Each of these specks contains an entire galaxy of stars. The distance between each galaxy is astronomical. It is believed that there are at least a billion galaxies contained in the universe. Some galaxies are larger, others with less stars than exists in the Milky Way. The universe is believed to have begun 13.7 billion years ago. Each star came into existence instantaneously, causing a bang or "pop," on its arrival.

In 1965, two scientists, employed by AT&T Bell Laboratories in New Jersey, discovered that radiation was at a constant level in every possible direction far beyond the Milky Way galaxy. This discovery opened a new door into space research. Following the radiation path, it is now possible to measure the actual size and even the shape of the universe. It has been determined that the universe extends 80 billion trillion miles in each direction from the earth. The two physicists, Penyias and Wilson, were awarded the Nobel Prize in 1978 for their discovery.

Efforts to discover what lies beyond the universe has ended in failure. Attempts to pry beyond the universe in all directions have resulted in abrupt halts due to an unseen wall that engulfs the entire universe, and it cannot be penetrated. The wall cannot be penetrated because there is no other place to go. Albert Einstein was correct. Physical matter does not exist beyond this universe, not even space. Space and time belong to the physical world.

Stars are beyond number, each radiating enormous energy. We earthlings realize that fuel is essential for life and that fuel is of a short duration. Highly refined fuel is required to place shuttles into orbit. In order to obtain a speed of 25,000 mph, necessary to orbit in space, it required 830 tons of fuel, which was contained in a fifteen-story high external tank. The powerful rocket engines consumed the fuel within moments (*Entering Space* by Joseph P. Allen, pg. 31).

While humans in every corner of the world struggled to obtain sufficient fuel, the stars beyond number have energy that last seemingly forever. Without warning, without a sign or disclosure suddenly stars are born. Our sun is one of the stars. It would require 1.3 million earths to equal the volume of our sun. Yet there are stars so large that if one of the largest was to trade places with the sun, Mercury, Venus, Earth, Mars, Jupiter and Saturn would be confined within the one star. There is no logical physical explanation for what exists, and the stars never need added fuel.

The Bible does not state that God had created the universe in one day. However, in the beginning He began with just two people. When that beginning was, is not stated. We do know that earth's time was regulated by the sun. As the earth moves around the sun, the seasons are produced. As we journey around the sun, the earth is turning around on its axis. This rotation causes night and day. The sun had to exist first. The first day had not begun until Genesis 1:5, when the sun introduced the first day. "The evening and the morning was the first day."

Earth is one of nine planets that circle the sun. Mercury, the closest planet to the sun is so hot that metal would flow like water.

The back side of the same planet untouched by the sun's radiation would remain frozen at a temperature of 459 degrees below absolute zero.

Venus is earth's closest neighbor and the hottest planet in the solar system. It has mountains higher than Mt. Everest and an atmosphere that contains a crushing pressure. It is hidden under a blanket of devastating acid clouds. In the 1960s, Russia was determined to be the first nation to place a mechanical machine on Venus. Six separate attempts were made without success. In each of these missions, the crafts were crushed by the pressure and possibly melted by the acid. On the seventh attempt, the Russian space craft was able to land the first successful mission to planet Venus.

On the opposite side of Earth is the planet Mars. Half the size of the Earth and it is dry and rocky. Its average temperature lingers near -65ºC. With an atmosphere two hundred times thinner than what exists on Earth, the air on Mars would be poisonous if there was enough to air to breath. The rocky terrain is covered with a thick, red volcanic dust that frequently lingers as clouds and is driven by strong winds that cover the entire planet. The lack of atmosphere allows the sun's ultraviolet rays to scorch Mars's surface. Its canyons are immense having a depth equal to Mt. Everest's height.

Jupiter is the fifth planet from the sun and is the largest in the solar system. 1,321 earths could easily fit inside Jupiter's volume. Gigantic flashes of lightning dash over the planet as strong and steady winds blow in alternate directions of speed of 640 meters per second. Jupiter's exterior has a pressure of over two million times the air pressure that exists on Earth. Jupiter has the largest number of moons in our solar system. By the year 2004, sixty-three satellites were discovered to orbit Jupiter.

Saturn is the second largest planet in the solar system. Similar to Jupiter, intense heat exists at its core while it's exterior remains at minus 240ºF. Powerful winds blow five hundred meters per second and Saturn's distinguishing feature is its brilliant appearance in the night sky. This is due to seven rings that consist of thousands of ringlets. The rings are made of dust like specks to boulder the size of automobiles. What makes these rings even more spectacular is that each of the rings orbits Saturn at a different speed. Spacecraft that wanders too closely could easily become part of those scenic rings.

Pluto, one-fifth of the size of Earth is so small and distant from both the sun and the Earth, that it is was not discovered until 1930. Pluto has one moon, Charon and is similar in size to Pluto. Pluto is intensely cold at minus 225ºC. and is so distant from the sun that each of its orbits around the sun requires 248 years.

With the moon, there exists a bond that unites the moon to planet Earth. The moon's influence over the Earth is major. The moon's gravitational pull causes the oceans to move twice a day. The moon influences the mood within the mind and spirit on both man and beast. Its influence on the lives of people, animals and even plants is substantial. The moon serves as a shield over the Earth. Major hits from space objects would have caused havoc on Earth, except for the moon. The moon is riddled with craters caused by direct hits from space matter.

The moon has no light or heat of its own. Rather the moon reflects light from the sun. Airless, dry, rocky, cold, it is a dead and forbidding world. Yet the moon is the brightest object in the night sky. The moon arouses romance to the lover, inspires song and poetry to the composer; the navigator is able to chart a course though the darkest night. The night animal would have no sight but for the light of the moon.

Adam said to his bride, "This is now bone of my bones and flesh of my flesh." This cannot be said in referring to the moon's relationship with Earth. Lunar rocks removed from the moon look the same as stones on Earth but differ considerably in their elements. The moon's surface is covered in a fine-grained material named, "regolith." Moon dust is a dead rock substance in which nothing can grow (National Geographic Encyclopedia of Space, page 141). Due to the lack of atmosphere, sound is nonexistent on the moon. Stars are nowhere to be seen and the sky is continually black. In the distance, a quarter of a million miles away, astronauts saw a visible object. The only object that was shining in the darkness was the Earth.

Chapter 2

The Earth

Facing the sun is Mercury and Venus. They are so hot that copper would flow like melted butter. On Earth's opposite side exists Mars with five unfriendly cohorts. All six of those planets remain so cold that no life could exist.

Earth's distance from the sun is 92.96 million miles and brilliantly placed. However, the distance from the Earth to the sun is not the end of the story. Without a proper atmosphere, no life could survive on planet Earth. The sun's violent release of radiation would soon turn Earth into another Venus. One hundred tons of space dust is claimed to fall on earth each day. After a room is cleaned and dusted with window closed, doors shut and without an occupant. Within a few days the room will again be covered with dust.

Air is without color, yet the sky appears blue. This is caused by the constant flow of falling dust from the sky. Meteoroids may be mistakenly identified as falling stars. In reality, it was a metal or stone object hurtling through space at a great speed. As it enters the earth's atmosphere, it is destroyed in a brilliant flash of light.

Earth's amazing atmosphere transfers sound from one human to another. Think of life without a song, radio, or sound. On the moon exists dead silence. Earth's atmosphere carries sound, filters the sun's dangerous radiation and holds heat on the earth's surface. It protects Earth from a barrage of space particles and supplies breath for our lungs.

Water is one of Earth's essential substances. Water alone has no power to produce life. While water is required to maintain life, nearly 70 percent of the world is covered by water. The majority of the earth's water is undrinkable for humans. Drinking saltwater can lead to death. Liquid is no guarantee to sustain life. The Dead Sea is a large body of water so salty that no life exists in it.

There exists a coherence between the sun and earth's atmosphere that allows light to thrive on earth. The sun's radiation heats the earth's surface which allows the atmosphere to lift the invisible moisture and in doing so rejects impure pollutions. The pure vapors form clouds that become heavy with moisture, distributing water in the form of rain over the earth. Sections of earth that receive little or no rain become deserts.

Earth's atmosphere not only purifies our water, but the falling rain cleanses the air we breathe. Dust and pollutions become proteins for vegetation. "Oh, how sweet is the air we breathe after a spring rain."

Dirt is among the many miracles that support life. Nothing is greater than what lies beneath our feet. Name it dust, earth, or just plain dirt. It's what we are made of. Everything on earth or in the sea that has life is a product produced from soil. Fish, fowl, animal, or man left on earth to die, returns to its natural origin of dust. The foundation food, for all creatures is the land. From the earth we were created; earth is our only food source and to the earth will our bodies return. A bucket of soil has no value to a starving man or creature. Yet every tiny seed contains the ability to feed itself and others, using the soil.

The contents of an egg cannot be duplicated by man. Left in its shell under the proper heat, the contents will turn into flesh, bone, feathers, and life. No one is able to explain or manufacture life. We are able to send a man to the moon, explain the universe, and reveal what we think happened billions of years ago, but the seed, the soil beneath our feet remains a mystery.

The Earth's exterior is on display for all to witness. Hidden in the interior, earth has a wealth of amazing goods. Iron ore, aluminum, copper, zinc, uranium, silver, gold, salt, coal for fuel, gas, oil, and water—all organic products manufactured from the earth for use on the earth.

Coal is harvested from a depth hundreds of feet below earth's surface, causing a cavity hundreds of feet in all directions. Salt is essential for the existence of life, used to preserve food for seasoning and health. Without salt, people have been willing to work, paid in wages using salt. As coal, salt is mined in huge underground cavities. One salt mine spreads under Detroit and is so large that it is said to be like a city beneath a city.

Water does not produce salt. There are thousands of lakes scattered over the world, few have slat water, most have fresh water. Lake Michigan, Lake Huron, and Lake Superior are all large bodies containing fresh water. Salt Lake City has a moderate size lake that is salty. Rivers and brooks are not all fresh water; some flow with salt water. Gila River in Arizona is salty, and a salty river flows in South Carolina. Water left in a clean container may become stagnant but never salty. Oceans have become salty not from the air, size, or age, rather, due to the fact that they are located on a field of salt in the earth.

Petroleum is deep within the confinements of the earth. There is a wealth of oil and gas. Millions of gallons of petroleum are removed from the depths of the earth on a daily basis. The proponents of evolution explain petroleum as a natural process that occurred as a result of the death of millions of creatures and the decay of vegetation.

Whales that are stranded on land, as with all creatures large or small. In death, they return to dust. They do not leave even an ounce of oil to mark their death. This is also true of vegetation that returns to the earth. The popular myth of petroleum's origin may have appeared as true many years ago. However, today with petroleum proven to exist in massive quantities, it should be obvious to all that petroleum within the earth is a marvel which is manufactured in the earth and by the earth itself.

Flesh, fat, and vegetation is reduced to oil while the product is fresh. The oil used from food products is essential for cooks and can promote good health. The oil removed from the earth, if swallowed will be a person's demise. The oil excreted from food lacks the durability required by machinery or modern automobiles. To meet the required demand of machines, oil from food is fortified using natural oils from the earth.

Evolutionists inform us that Earth is the result of numerous hot projectiles slammed together with such vigorous force that a fusion bonded the elements into a hot ball. Millions of years were required for earth's surface to cool. Such a summary of events would guarantee a sterilized planet, and that planet would remain as an empty rock, on a useless journey around a sun that shines without purpose!

Chapter 3

✳ ✱ ✳ ✱ ✳

Before Adam

There are statements in the Bible that inform us that before Adam, there existed thriving nations on earth. The Prophet Jeremiah was admonished by God to warn the people that the people who once existed no longer exists due to their behavior. God can do the same thing again! In a vision, Jeremiah witnessed the destruction of the previous world.

> "I beheld the earth and indeed it was without form
> and void; and the heavens, they had no light. I beheld
> the mountains, and indeed they trembled, and all the
> hills moved back and forth. I beheld, and indeed there
> was no man, and all the birds of the heavens had fled.
> I beheld, and indeed the fruitful land was a wilderness,
> and all its cities were broken down at the presence of
> the Lord. By His fierce anger." (Jeremiah 4:22–26)

Notice the similar wording of to the Genesis account. Genesis states; "The earth was without form and void; and darkness was on the face of the deep. And the Spirit of God was hovering over the face of the waters" (Genesis 1:2). The Genesis account is the condition that existed when God returned to restore the devastated earth, void of all life. Jeremiah's account is the opposite from Noah's flood. In Noah's flood, seven humans replenished the earth. A male and a female of every creature survived at the time of Noah's flood. Jeremiah reported that all life had vanished, including its great forests and cities had become a desert.

In the book of Job, we discover a very rich and proud man who considered himself perfect and righteous in his walk with God and among man. Hard times fell on Job because of illness, friends and family problems. Job turned on God, accusing God for his many problems.

Job informed God that he (Job) was an honorable man. That he had accomplished many good deeds and it was wrong for God to treat him with such distain. Jobs rant against God continued for some time. Then, God answered Job. "Job, where were you when I made the earth? Where were you when I measured the earth's size? Where you there to stretch the line or to hold the earth in its place? Who made the sea or said to the water, you may go so far, but no further?"

Then God named creatures that once roamed the earth, but no longer exists. "Do you know the behemoth, or the leviathan? Large dreadful animals, who as you Job, were made of flesh and blood." Job had no knowledge of their historical past.

Fossil remains of extinct creatures have been discovered in every continent, except for Antarctica, which remains under ice. The myth of their demise in Noah's flood is wrong. Noah was required to preserve a male and female of every animal. The remnants from that boat still exist. But where are all the dinosaurs?

Individual creatures from the dinosaur age are on occasions found. Most discoveries are in massive graves containing hundreds of skeletons of animals that once roamed the earth. Creatures that were bitter enemies, others so timid that they would avoid other species. Yet for this occasion, all creatures large or small, friend or enemies died together. All met death in the same period of time and in the same manner. On each other they lay, twisted, tangled together—not as in battle, but victims to circumstances beyond their control.

Had their climacteric end been the result of a large meteorite, or a stellar explosion as suggested, bodies would have been torn apart and scattered in varied location. The very opposite occurred. A force lifted and carried unwilling creatures into a gully where they became embalmed by mud and debris in heaps together.

The mystery of the vanished dinosaur world is revealed in the very first chapter of the Bible. In the second verse, we discovered that the entire earth was submerged beneath the waters.

> "And the Spirit of God moved upon the
> face of the water." (Gen. 1:2)

In the beginning, God had created a perfect earth, not a body of water. The original earth was a world of plenty and of beauty. Genesis is the story of redemption, the story of restoration from a world that had been cursed, buried beneath the water. The entire earth had become a sea.

Darwin

Charles Darwin, not the most ambitious of humans, was encourage by his parents to become a priest or minister. Such a title, they thought, would provide Charles with security and prestige. Charles also had a very ambitious grandfather who was both a physician and a scientist. Granddads words deeply influenced young Charles. Dr. Erasmus Darwin was the originator of the theory of evolution.

In 1827, Charles enrolled as a divinity student in the Cambridge University where he studied for three long years. Charles disliked his studies; however, he could not forget the second verse of the Bible: "and the spirit of God moved upon the face of the waters." The concept that the earth was possibly conceived under water lingered in Darwin's thoughts. Having a false concept, Darwin began his classic myth of how life evolved from under the sea.

Without a clue as to how the earth came into being, the distinguished world of science united with this theory as absolute truth. The "Big Bang" theory, which they also embrace, implied the very opposite!

The earth began as a result of a burning umber that discharged from the Big Bang. Burning bits of matter thrown from the explosion, bonded to the umber which eventually became the earth. Millions of years were required for the burned out matter to cool. In fact, the fire still burns as volcanoes vent their apparent anger to earth's surface.

Extreme heat can cause sterilization. Regardless of known facts in regard to sterilization, people hold to their adopted opinion. Coal is a solid rock that is used as fuel. Once the fuel valve has burned out, what remains are ashes. The rock may not have diminished in quantity, but the cinders are used as fill beneath walkways where undesired weeds would otherwise grow. The cinder will never again regain new life. Had the earth been conceived in fire as claimed, the sterilized earth could never support life. And that is a scientific fact!

Chapter 4

✻ ✳ ✼ ✳ ✻

God's Garden

Overture

"In the beginning, God created the heaven's and the earth."

How God created or when God created remains in total silence. Fictitious stories can be told that illustrate valid logic. Not hearing directly from God, I offer this version of what could have transpired during creation. In the language and imagination of a child, this is "God's Garden."

It's not easy being God. When someone has always existed, new ideas can become scarce. God had decided that he would build a new universe. Heaven is grand but, how about something totally unique?

God had a plan but told no one. God began by making stars. So many stars that the angels stopped counting. God's new universe had an assortment of objects that were hurling in every direction. The angels inquired amongst themselves, "What's the purpose of all this stuff?"

Angels served as God's only audience and God heard their conversation. God announced the purpose for such a grand creation. God was to cultivate a garden. "A garden inquired the angels?" Yes, a garden, and in that garden would live a being similar to the angels.

This news excited the heavens. "The stars sang together, and the angels shouted with joy" (Job 38:7). King David said, "The heavens declare the glory of God" (Ps. 19:1–4).

The angels gathered together to witness the spectacle that required so grand a creation. Then God's hand reached in among the stars and took what appeared as a small amount of clay. He rolled that clay into a round ball. God hurled that ball toward the sun. Between Venus and mars that ball lodged, bound by an invisible cord to the sun.

Around and around the earth circled around the sun in a relentless journey. Drops of sweat from the master's brow fell on the clay, and those drops became streams and the streams became rivers that journeyed across the earth. Moisture from those drops caused vegetation to spout. A blanket of vegetation became so dense that the naked earth hid from the sun and God's breath became the air that we breathe.

Earth inhabited by creatures of every description wandered the plains, swim the waters, and ascend into the air. Despite the splendor of such a grand creation, the purpose of earth alluded the angels. Then, in the fullness of time, a godlike creature was created, unique from the animal kingdom. This being, was equipped with the capability to govern the earth!

Lucifer

God always appoints a supervisor who oversees and executes God's program. Among the many qualified angels, there appeared to be a consensual agreement that an angel named Lucifer would be the most qualified to handle God's garden.

In accordance to the ancient Hebrew language, Lucifer meant "the shining one." Never in existence had there been a being whose appearance was superior to that of Lucifer. The Bible states the Lucifer was "perfect in beauty." Not only perfect in appearance, Lucifer was also smart—"full of wisdom." Lucifer was the "model and seal of perfection," "perfect in every detail from the day of his creation" (Ezek. 28:12–17).

Accompanied with a sizable number of angels, Lucifer assumed responsibility for the earth under God's authority. God's garden was a beautiful and perfect planet. Evil nor death were part of the equation. Thorns nor thistles were not part of the earth's inventory. Oceans that divided nations were not in existence. Earth's temperature was ideal, and its people were good.

As centuries past, Lucifer began to change. Lots of work but lacking on praise. Why should he do all the work and God gets all the glory. Also, Lucifer's angels piled heaps of praise on Lucifer's ability as a leader. It is "I, thought Lucifer, not God who dominates over the earth." Who is able to equal my greatness." This inherent pride may have existed in Lucifer to some degree, but now in this exalted position, pride exceeded his intelligence (Isaiah 14:12–17).

Lucifer began to encourage adoration for himself rather than to God. Gradually this impulse grew to the extent that Lucifer believed himself to be God's equal. Lucifer together with his angels would one day become so obstinate with the thought of power, that they invade heaven expecting to dominate over God. Instead Lucifer and his angels (demons) were cast from heaven to the earth where they will remain until they are thrown into Hell. Open hostility became obvious. "I am god claimed Lucifer as he incited ridicule against what he once called holy."

Abuse replaced kindness. Mischief was substituted for integrity. Children were misused, mislead morally, and even killed. Belief in the true God disappeared. All types of apostasies became popular and no one was willing to acknowledge faith in the true God. Torture of animals and of humans became common as a sacrifice to their invented deity's.

The Consequence of a Depraved World

It was midday that the sun began to fade. The sky eventually vanished unlike any previous day known to mankind. Lanterns were lit; the black sky bulged heavy with moisture. The sky, unable to contain its water, burst open on a bewildered earth.

The water gushed on the earth as if a tank of water had burst over a nest. All that night the torrential rains continued; through the day, the night and the next day. The relentless torrents of rain would not stop. The earth vanished beneath the water and earth was transformed into a sea.

The rain ended, and the sun looked down from the clear blue sky. Silence hung over earth's demise. Not the song of a bird, not the movement of a creature could be heard; there was no one to witness God's vengeance on an evil world (Heb. 10:30).

A Quiver?

Certainly, the silence was a good omen. The worst had past when a quiver stirred the waters. After a pause, another quiver, then another. Each quiver increased with intensity. Something in the earth was causing a calamity. Earth's rumbles became so intense as if the entire earth would split into pieces.

From beneath the water rose sections of the earth. God's beautiful earth was being torn apart. From beneath the water rose mountains. Then from below the sea rose huge monsters spitting fire, smoke, and molten rock into the atmosphere.

The birth of volcanoes shot dust particles into the sky where they drifted into the earth's atmosphere. This infestation of burned particles saturated earth's atmosphere causing the earth to become embalmed in darkness. The dark ominous atmosphere drifted many miles above the earth, eliminating the sun's rays from penetrating the earth. Earth would remain in total darkness until God's voice shattered the night, stating, "Let there be light."

An Ice Age?

Unlike a pot-belly stove that heats air on all sides, the sun heats through radiation. Planets near the sun burn with extreme heat. The side of a rock exposed to the sun is extremely hot. The back side of the same rock will remain ice cold. The sun's rays continued to shine brightly elsewhere but the earth embalmed in a heavy black atmosphere concealed the earth from the suns light. When God came to restore the earth, the earth had lost its original form, void of life and under total darkness.

Venus is closer to the sun than the earth and has a constant temperature that would melt lead. The opposite side of Venus remains in total darkness having a temperature of one to two hundred degrees below the freezing point. Mars exists on earth's further side from the sun and on its dark side also has a temperature of one to two hundred degrees below 32ºF. Draped under the covers of a very dark polluted atmosphere, the earth rejected the sun's light plunging earth into total darkness and under water. The water became a hardened ball of ice.

Chapter 5

✳ ✳ ✳ ✳ ✳

The Six Days of Creation

God looked down and remembered earth.

> "The earth was without form, and void; darkness
> was on the face of the deep. The Spirit of God
> moved over the face of the waters. And God said,
> "Let there be light and there was light." (Gen. 1:3)

The darkness began to vanish, and light reappeared on the earth. Darkness had rejected the light. Now at God's command, the poisonous atmosphere vanished. With the disappearance of earth's polluted atmosphere, the sun's rays would rival the heat as exists on Venus. The ice would soon melt, and the earth would assume its former state as a flooded planet.

Earth's Journey

God divided the light from the darkness. God called the light "day," and He called the darkness "night." Earth, in its movements, has remained similar from the day of creation. The earth moves around the sun at speeds of approximately 18.5 miles per second, a journey that results in the four seasons. Summer, fall, winter, and spring.

In addition, "God divided the light from the darkness." God caused this divide by placing a spin on the earth, turning in a motion known as rotation. Only one side of the earth is lit by the sun at a time. When we are on the bright side, it is daytime; when we are on the dark side, it is night.

No other object in the sky has a rotation, only the earth. There exists more planets and more moons than we are able to count, yet not one rotates in their journey. This is one of many provisions that qualifies only the earth as a suitable habituate for life. God reminds us that it was He, who divided the light from darkness.

The Second Day

Then God said, "Let there be a firmament in the midst of the waters and let it divide the waters from the waters." Thus, God made the firmament and divided the waters which were under the firmament from the waters which were above the firmament; and it was so (Genesis 1:6–8).

The sun's radiant heat had plundered the ice-covered earth with extravagant heat. Unrestricted by an atmosphere, the frozen earth quickly thawed. However, space void of atmosphere was unable to lift water from the earth. It was on this second day that God replenished earth's atmosphere. The old poisonous atmosphere had vanished, and in the absence of the atmosphere, water could not lift from the earth.

At God's command, a new pure air supply filled the vacuum causing huge quantities of moisture to lift towards the sky; so massive were the vapors, that the heavens could no longer be seen. "A mist went up from the earth" (Gen. 2:6). God had divided the waters that once occupied the earth by sending the excess into the heavens, causing the clouds to form.

The Third Day

God said, Let the waters under the heavens be gathered together into one place and let the dry land appear and it was so. God called the dry land Earth and the gathering together of the waters He called seas. God saw that it was good. Then God said, "Let the earth bring forth grass, the herb that yields seed and the fruit tree that yields fruit according to its kind, whose seed is in itself, on the earth," and it was so. The earth brought forth grass, the herb that yields seed according to its kind, and the tree that yields fruit, whose seed is in itself according to its kind. And God saw that it was good." (Genesis 1:9–13)

The first earth must have been an object of beauty. The majestic God who created a heaven with streets paved with gold, gates that exist from a single pearl. Earth, as God's garden must have been a wonder to behold. In each act of creation, God looked with pride, stating "that's good." Earth's beauty was such that it caused Lucifer, earth's guardian, pride.

Lucifer led the entire world in rebellion against God. In response, God lit fire in the earth's belly. Hell, a burning fire inside the earth where the wicked are sent after death. According, to the words of Jesus, hell is an everlasting fire. The fire became so immense that sections of earth lifted while other sections sank. Blow holes spouted fire, dense smoke, and lava. No longer the envy of the universe, earth would remain scarred until God again renews the earth at the end of the millennium (Rev. 21:1).

On the third day, God caused dry land to appear. The neat and tidy earth had become deformed. A pain that caused deep valleys, hills, and mountains to form. The hollows became ponds, lakes, and the grandest of them all became the oceans. The prevailing misconception is that each of the six days represents a twenty-four hours day. Day three is the one day that reveals each of the six days likely representing a period of time, not days consisting of twenty-four hours.

The atmospheric evaporation caused dry land to appear on this third day. Then in what remains of this third day, the earth is filled by mature forests and vegetation that cover the entire earth.

God's power to do so is not in question. The question remains, is that what took place? God had never created a group of men or a group of women. God created one of each, instructing them to multiply. Had God created a thousand oak trees at one time? He created one of each kind with the capacity to create many.

It was God who said:

> "Let the earth bring forth grass, the herb
> yielding seed, the fruit tree yielding
> fruit after his kind, whose seed is in itself."
> (Gen. 1:11–12)

When the entire creation was completed, on the seventh day, God rested.

> "Thus, the heavens and the earth,
> and all the host of them were finished."
> (Gen. 2:1)

After God's day of rest, after earth's completion, we discover that despite a number of days had passed, no new growth was visible.

> "Before any plant of the field was in
> the earth and before any herb of the
> field had grown…. A mist went up from
> the earth and watered the whole face of
> the ground." (Gen. 2:5–6)

God filled the earth with vegetation by natural growth. God had placed the exact detailed plan of what a seed would become when planted into the earth. The miracle was in the seed and only God can create a seed.

Long before there was an Adam, earth itself was endowed with an abundant harvest of vegetation. The earth became submerged beneath the waters. All vegetation died. Had the seed lingered under water it would have rotted. Had there been no water and the seed exposed to many years of constant radiant heat, the seed would have disintegrated. The earth became frozen in ice, preserving the seed.

When God commanded the earth to bring forth, the seed instantly came to life and began its normal growth.

What is understood by the word "day"?

The word day can be used as applying to several circumstances. Twenty-four hours is one day. Day is the opposite of night. A blessing is implied when stating, "have a good day." During "Moses day" refers to his 120 years. "In the day that the Lord God made the earth and the heavens" (Gen. 5:1–2). The earth and the heavens were not created in one day. Adam was told not to eat the fruit from one specific tree. "In the day, you eat of that tree you shall surely die" (Gen. 2:17). Adam ate from the tree and died 930 years later, Peter states: "Be not ignorant of this one thing, that one day is with the Lord as a thousand years, and a thousand years as one day" (2 Peter 3:8). Could Peter be referring to the six days of creation?

Genesis 2:5 clearly states, that time was required for the seed to grow. If each of those days represented twenty-four hours, a major disaster would happen on days five and six. On those days, all the earth's creatures would come into existence on a naked earth empty of food. Each of the six days represents a period of time, required for the event to be completed. The day ended only when God saw that what he had created, "was very good."

Strange that God's miracles are not always instantaneous. Frequently, prayers are answered in such a natural manor that often we are left in confusion. "Was it God or of natural causes?"

The Bible begins by stating how the universe and life came into existence. Such a huge story told in very few words. No explanation as to how, when, or why. Both sinner and saint alike have wrestled with these words in disagreement from the day Moses wrote them. Thousands of years have now past, and the text still remains disputed. Despite, disagreements from each new generation, no voice has been able to disprove the accuracy of the Hebrew Christian Bible.

The Fourth Day

God said, "Let there be light in the firmament of
the heavens to divide the day from the night; and
let them be for signs and seasons, and for days,
and years; and let them be for lights in the firmament
of the heavens to give light on the earth; and it was so.
Then God made two great lights; the greater light to
rule the day, and the lesser light to rule the night.
He made the stars also. God set them in the firmament
of the heaven to give light on the earth, and to rule over
the day and over the night, and to divide the light from
the darkness." (Gen. 1:14–19)

The language is such that it can easily be misunderstood. When language is translated from one language to another; the original text becomes a version by an author of what the original text is stating. Several translations of the same text may vary, but not to distort, the inherent intent.

No, we do not believe that the earth is flat. Neither do we believe that the earth is held in place by a huge elephant. Further, we do not believe that the universe is the result of an accident. The stars as was the sun were not created on the fourth day. As stated in the text, the heavens were created in the beginning of time. Possibly millions of years before the fourth day.

Genesis 2:6 states that a mist watered the whole earth. The seed grew under ideal conditions, constant moisture rather than rain. Heat without the sun's direct radiation. The prevailing fog was so dense that the sky hid its face from the earth. Today, we consider the dispersing of fog as a normal event. On that fourth day, God lifted the moisture from off the earth causing clouds to form. This atmospheric change gave visibility to the heavens above. The heavens that were visible in the beginning lost that visibility due to a polluted atmosphere.

The restoration of the atmosphere restored the view of the heavens to those who one day would exist on earth. Life on earth would be new, while the heavens and the objects in the heavens would remain as they had existed from their beginning.

Approximately three thousand years ago, King Solomon wrote:

"There is nothing new under the sun.
Is there anything that can be said,
Look! This is something new?" It was
already, long ago." (Ecclesiastes 1)

The Fifth Day

God said, "Let the waters abound with an abundance
of living creatures and let birds fly above the earth across
the face of the firmament of the heavens." So, God
created great sea creatures and every living thing that
moves with which the waters abounded, after their kind,
and every winged bird after its kind. And God saw that it
was good. And God blessed them saying, "Be fruitful and
multiply, and fill the waters in the seas, and let birds multiply
on the earth." (Genesis 1:20–23)

Had the length of each day represented twenty-four hours, the many millions of creatures that appeared on day five and six would have had no food (Genesis 2:5–6). The Bible states that the seed on day three had not yet grown.

Surely creation reveals God as having a sense of humor. He created great massive whales to minute insects that are scarcely visible. Creatures that exist in devious depths of the sea and confined to distinctive types of water. God made the beautiful peacock and the ugly spider. Creatures exist that have never been seen by mortal man. Yet no creature exists that God has not made.

In the story of humankind, we discovered that God made only one man and one woman. A group of people were not created, only one male and one female with instructions to multiply and fill the earth. These instructions were not orally given, rather the words imply an inherent nature that was given, to multiply.

This same procedure likely existed throughout the creation on earth. A flock of geese were not created, rather a single male and female goose that had the desire to mate. This basic principle can also be applied to vegetation. God had not created a forest of oak trees. He created one oak tree with the capacity to propagate thousands of trees in its own likeness.

Vegetation had previously covered the earth. Its seed from that day lingered within the earth so that no new vegetation was required to produce seed. God spoke to that seed to "bring forth" and God saw that it was good.

The Sixth Day

Then God said, "Let the earth bring forth the living creature according to its kind; cattle and creeping thing and beast of the earth, each according to its kind," and it was so. And God made the beast of the earth according to its kind, cattle according to its kind, and everything that creeps on the earth after its kind. And God saw that it was good.

Then God said, "Let Us make man in Our image, according to Our likeness; let them have dominion over the fish of the sea, over the birds of the air, and over the cattle, over all the earth and over every creeping thing that creeps on the earth." So, God created man in His own image, in the image of God He created him; male and female He created them. Then Gold blessed them, and God said to them, "Be fruitful and multiply, fill the earth and subdue it; have dominion over the fish of the sea, over the birds of the air, and every living thing that moves on the earth" (Genesis 1:24–28).

If one day was to represent twenty-four hours, then day six would fall short to accomplish all that is stated. On that day, God created each creature that either creeps, walks, or flies, then made humankind.

Chapter 2 details the appearance of Adam and Eve. Verse 7 informs us that God made Adam from earth's dust. When that body was completed, God blew breath into the nostrils of man, and Adam became a living soul. We know this to be true; when a human stops breathing, they return to their natural origin of dust.

Adam awoke to life in a garden, filled with trees bursting with a ripe harvest. Hunger instinctively caused him to reach for fruit, but without a teacher, he had to learn that the peel on an orange or the peel of a banana was not good. And what good is a coconut? Adam soon learned that he could not walk on water and that there existed an entire world that he knew nothing about.

Eventually, in some manner, God corresponded with Adam and taught him how to cultivate, maintain, and care for the garden. Eventually, God added a new job to Adams agenda. "Provide a name to each beast of the field and every bird in the air." Adam must have had a very exceptional and brilliant mind because Adam, gave names to cattle, birds and to each living creature. Whatever Adam named them remained their true names.

Adam studied the animal life. He witnessed the distinctions between male and female. He witnessed the birth of creatures and had a basic understanding of the principles. When God created a woman from Adam's rib, Adam instantly knew the implication and distinction between male and female. The first words spoken by a human still can be heard and remain true.

"This is now bone of my bones and flesh of my flesh;
she shall be called woman, for she was taken out of man."
For this reason, a man will leave his father and mother
and be united to his wife, and they will become one flesh."

Both, male and female were created in the same period of time on the sixth day. Adam's day may have exceeded Eve's day by a few years. Adam was created first and from his body came the substance to form Eve. This remains true to this day. From the male comes the life germ that causes life to develop.

Less is written of Eve than Adam in the Bible, despite the fact that she remains one of the two most important women to ever exist. She is the mother of us all. Some would argue that Mary, the mother of Jesus was the most important woman. However, without Eve, there would be no Mary!

Minor facial changes and skin color began at the tower of Babel, approximately 2,300 BC. Despite these changes, we remain one blood, one flesh, a distinct human rise from the same origin and parent, Adam and Eve.

In the act of creation, each creature was distinct but limited by its own kind. Not a hint of one species gradually becoming another species. Repeatedly God stressed that each living creature whether in the sea, land, or in the air, was to multiply to fill the earth with his own kind.

Humans have repeatedly attempted to pregnant animals by the use of semen fluid from a different species without success. To the bewilderment of evolutionary proponents, each species is limited to its own kind. However, variations within a species is common. One of the most familiar variations is the dog species. Small as a Pekingese or as large as a Saint Bernard.

If all creatures including man, had originated from a single source, a common link would exist in all creatures, but that is not the case. Man is not elevating into a higher species, nor is there a creature almost man. Fossils remain extinct from the dinosaur age. Fossil remains stay true in their silent witness that throughout all of earth's history, not a single creature has revealed a process of change from one species to another. Yet there are those who are willing to lie, in order to advance their cause.

God's Image

God created humankind in his own image. Yet God is invisible, we are not. God is everywhere at the same time. We are confined by a physical body. God created the universe from nothing. We are unable to duplicate the acts of God. In what respect do we bear God's image?

Creatures of the earth lack the ability to reason. No animal questions the number of stars or whether there is a God. Animals seldom are seen in church and never pray. Human intellect is considerably beyond the animal kingdom despite those who insist that humans are animals.

Only humans have the awareness that a God exists. Historically, humans have always believed in a spirit world. The sculpturing of idols, building temples and worship centers do so in recognition of a being that we are unable to see. It is this awareness and divinely inspired intellect that empowers humanity to dominate over the animal kingdom and to dominate over the earth.

"Male and Female He created them" (Gen. 1:27).

God made one of each kind. One is unable to multiply and fill the earth as God commanded. Two were required—both different in style and design. One is incomplete, unable to duplicate the actions of the other. Together, the two form a bond that equals one.

Even vegetation that includes grass and weeds do not grow in seclusion. All flowers, fruit, and vegetables are the combined chemical union that results in the male and female aspect of creation. Seed to grow plants require pollen. Pollen is a fine dust like mass that contains the male sexual cells necessary to produce life.

A male and female is required to produce all water creatures. Regardless of size, each insect or animal that walks, creeps, swims, or flies, requires male and female to produce its own kind. The male is not completely apart from the female, nor is the female qualified to raise children apart from the male. God had not invented sex for the purpose of fun and games. Sex was created as the exclusive means to fill the earth with its own kind. The sexual drive was intended to force male and female together in a sacred marriage.

"Therefore, a man shall leave his father and mother
be joined to his wife and they shall become one flesh." (Gen. 2:24)

The home, marriage and sex, is for the exclusive purpose and benefit of having children. Unfortunately, this law of God is being excluded and the world is reaping a harvest of an undisciplined world. The home is in shambles and many consider marriage as obsolete. Today, men enjoy all the benefits of sex without the responsibility of marriage. Children wander the streets looking for excitement and, in some schools, children are taught how to have sex without a pregnancy.

Those who believe that we are the descendants of animals, also believe that the world is moving forward to a higher development of maturity, and that religion has hindered the development of modern man.

Unfortunately, the love of self-rule, the denial of the true God, and insisting that we are gods, is the same reasoning that led to the demise of the old world. The same evil that had a firm hold in the past has revived. The "Grim Reaper" has his foot in the door and desires entrance. What was once morally depraved behavior has now become normal, and those who oppose today's standards are considered as prudes.

The Seventh Day

"By the seventh day God had finished the work He had been doing; on the seventh day He rested from all his work. God blessed the seventh day and made it holy, because on it He rested from all the work of creating that he had done" (Gen. 2:1–3).

"In the beginning, God created." When the beginning started, remains unknown despite numerous claims. Those proceeding millions of years that may have existed, are ignored in the book of Genesis. However, the remains of a past world reappear. God restored the earth that bears the scarred remains of a distant past.

The seventh day was distinct from the previous six days. Each of the six days represents a period of time. The clock measures a day as twelve hours. One day and a night is twenty-four hours. Adam's day was 930 years. Each of the six days as measured by what was accomplished.

Only moments were required for God to command earth to "bring forth." The oak tree can shed its seed in moments. For the seed to produce a forest, it requires years. God's day was completed when "God saw that it was good."

God was so delighted with His completed work that He signified the event with a special blessing. God announced that the seventh day was to be a Sabbath, a holy day unto the Lord. The represented cycle of seven-day weeks has no logical reasoning as to why it exits apart from the Bible. God made the cycle of a seven-day week, and this holds true worldwide.

> "Six days may work be done; but in the seventh
> is the Sabbath of rest, holy to the Lord: Whosoever
> doeth any work in the Sabbath day, he shall surely
> be put to death." (Exodus 31:15)

The observance of God's day of rest was regarded as an honored obligation in both the Old and New Testaments. Jesus was accused of violating the Sabbath on several occasions. When He and His disciples picked and ate corn on the Sabbath (Matthew 12:1). Jesus healed a man who had a withered hand on the Sabbath day (Matt. 12:10–14).

Jesus responded with a question. "If your animal fell into a pit on the Sabbath, would you not pull it out? Is it wrong to do a good deed on the Sabbath?" Jesus then made a very profound statement. Jesus claimed to be greater than the Sabbath, and that the Sabbath was made for man, not man for the Sabbath (Mark 2:27–28).

Jesus laid silent in the tomb on the seventh day. On the first day of the week, Jesus rose from the grave. The first day of the week became known as the "Lord's day" (Rev. 1:10). Hence, a divide separated God's people. Those who insist that the seventh day remains the true Sabbath. Others claim, that the true intent of the Sabbath can be celebrated in union with Christs day of resurrection. This disagreement has never been resolved.

The observance of the Sabbath in the mosaic legislation was to be observed by all and was strictly enforced. The observance of the Sabbath is one of the Ten Commandments written by God Himself on two tablets of stone given to Moses. The Ten Commandments will always point to perfection and true Followers of God. Christendom will always strive to observe one day a week out of respect for God.

Chapter 6

✴ ⁕ ✴ ⁂ ✴

The Hidden Path that Leads to Heaven

"Enter by the narrow gate, for wide is the gate
and broad is the way that leads to destruction,
and there are many who go in by it. Because
narrow is the gate and difficult is the way which
leads to life, and there are few who find it."
The words of Jesus. (Matt. 7:13–14)

Salvation: "A saving or being saved from danger, evil, difficulty, destruction, etc.; rescue" (*Webster's New World Dictionary*)

Innocence symbolized both Adam and Eve. Both were infants clothed in adult bodies. The earth was theirs. What their eyes were able to see was theirs, except for one tree. Touch it and you will die! Strange, that just one fruit tree among many, stood in the very center of God's garden with a warning, "Don't touch it, don't even go near to it or you will die!"

Within a few days, a foreign voice was heard calling from in the garden. "Who could that be?" thought Adam and Eve as they attempted to locate the voice. And indeed, the voice came from the center of God's garden and amazingly, from the forbidden tree! "Come over here my lovely one's" said the alluring voice. "The fruit of this tree is the finest in the garden. It's so good that God wants it all for Himself. This fruit will make you wise like God, knowing good and evil." Eve wanted to be wise, so she took the fruit ate of it and gave some to her husband who also ate the fruit.

Now Eve was unaware that snakes do not speak. She always had the ability to talk, why not snakes. Evil spirits at times are able to poses animals as well as human beings (Mk. 5:13). It was the devil who spoke out from the serpent. Do to the fact that a snake was used by the devil; snakes were cursed by God as the most despised in the animal Kingdom.

The Mystery of Sin

Why had God put such a tree in His garden, and why in such a prestigious location? Why were evil spirits allowed to exist on the new earth? Could a perfect angel become the devil in a trip from Heaven to the earth! Logic would require that a considerable length of years possibly millenniums were required for such an extreme change. This happened despite that angles are named as "Sons of God" (Gen. 6:20, Job 1:6).

The Gift of Choice

Why a tree of good and evil? No one could walk in the garden without seeing the tree. To add to man's excitement; there was a large snake in the garden that could talk! Each movement we make requires a choice. The hand does not move to the mouth without a choice. From the moment we wake, choices are involved in each movement. A wrong choice should never be repeated. Repetition creates habits difficult to manage.

God never lost control of His universe. God operates all things as He pleases. The devil exists on earth in order to temp and influence human behavior. My mother taught me that a good angel sits on one shoulder and an evil angel sits on the other shoulder. No good idea exists that is not challenged by negative thoughts. The battle between good and evil is constant. It is not God's will that any human should perish (Matt. 18:14). Despite God's best choice for each of us, He will not force His will on anyone person. God has created us with the freedom of choice. God planted a tree of good and evil so that humans could choose. God allowed a devil to exist as a choice. God had not created us as robots to worship Him night and day. The animal world has no choice, humans do. We do not serve God as a mechanism, but by choice. We may have the best of the devil's world or the choice to follow God. There is no third option.

The devil's world looks good for a brief moment. Is the alcoholic happy? Can those who habitually hunger for drugs find satisfaction? Pride led to Lucifer's downfall.

Pride is the very best Lucifer has to offer. He had promised that; you can do as you please and as often as you please. There are no restrictions. The lack of self-control is what divides true Christianity from those who suppose that they are in charge of their own destiny.

Thirty-six hundred years ago, Joshua spoke to a rebellious people. "Choose this day who would will serve" (Josh. 24:15). The choice was to decide who would rule over them? Would it be the Lord God who created all things, or the god of this world (the devil), who promised everything but created nothing. Today the questions remain the same. Who will I follow?

Evil versus Good

Evil existed even on the perfect earth. Satan and his agents were released on earth as a result of human disrespect for God's ordinance. Evil affected all forms of life. In a future day, Satan with his cohorts will be bound, locked in hell for a thousand years (Rev. 20:1–3). During the millennium, the earth will return to its former glory of perfection.

When that day arrives, animals will change from carnivores to grazing creatures. "The lion shall eat straw like the ox. The child shall play by the cobra's den without fear." Vegetation will flourish, free from disease, insects, even thorns (Isa. 11:6–9, 65:25). Human age will resort back prior to Noah's flood, when humans lived hundreds of years. Adam lived 930 years. Methuselah lived 969 years. During the millennium, those who die at the age of one hundred will be considered as children (Isa. 65:20).

Having superior bodies and long lives prior to Noah's flood, the number of births would have been enormous. The few names mentioned in the book of Genesis only do so to assist in teaching a lesson. They do not record the possibility of millions of people who existed on the earth from Adam to Noah's flood.

The Retrieve

In God's garden existed the tree of life. Those who ate from that tree would live forever. Being infected by sin, Adam and Eve were forced to leave the garden under the sentence of death. Instead of instant death, God granted a retrieve. God commuted their punishment by placing their crime on an innocent animal. God removed the skin from the dead animal and with its hide, made garments to cover the naked bodies of Adam and Eve.

Throughout the Bible, clothing has a spiritual implication. The priests were to be clothed in holy garments designed by God (Ex. 28). Each garment represented righteousness that covers the sinful body. In the Old Testament, physical clothing and numerous exercises were obligatory. In the New Testament garments represented God's righteousness that one day would cover the sins of the world. "Put on the Lord Jesus Christ" (Rom 13:14). "Put on the armor of light" (Rom.13:12). "Put on the whole armor of God" (Eph. 6:11).

The attempt to appease God by works in the Old Testament ended in a dismal failure. Dake's annotated reference Bible documents 2,345 commands that were additions to the book of the law Moses (page 113). It became an impossible task for any human including the priests, to obey all the laws and regulations demanded of the people.

On Jesus's arrival to earth, most of the church had become corrupt. Religion became a commercial enterprise. The priesthood became the police were the authorities of contagious diseases, sold animals used for sacrifice. The priest ruled all religious and civil matters in Jerusalem and became very unhappy because of the popularity bestowed on a new comer by the name of Jesus.

This Jesus was not a graduate of their philosophy. He had no holy robe, and He was not one of their recognized priests. Neither had he conformed to the rites and traditions of Judaism. This man was not one of them! Jesus was not crucified because of offense to the Roman government, rather, due to envy. Jealousy and pride caused holy men to become corrupt.

Animals are not man's equal in God's eyes. The death of an animal could not equal the death of a human life. When God said, "You will surely die." The death of an animal may temporarily deflect God's judgment, but by no means does it eliminate judgment. In ancient times, humans struggled to cleanse their souls from sin. Their appearance changed, but the threat of death lingered on. Can a leopard change its spots? Can a sinful man justify his soul by good works? All have sinned (Rom. 3:23). If we say that we have no sin, we deceive ourselves, and the truth is not in us (Jn. 1:8). What than can we say? When animal sacrifice fails, when good works are denied at heaven's gate, what then can we do?

Tradition

Many traditions are good, and some are vital. To substitute scripture for tradition is bad. Jesus accused the Pharisee priests of honoring tradition above or equal, to God's word. The finger of God wrote commands on stone then presented them to Moses. The clergy added many explanatory notes, massive rules so that the original script and the Pharisees advice became mingled. In their lectures to the public, the Pharisees notes were considered equal to the words from God. Jesus condemned these man-made traditions as not being God's equal (Mk. 7).

Noah's World

As the population of Adam's day increased, respect for God was in decline. Earth's massive population became extremely wicked. So wicked that Noah and his family were in danger as a result of a world under Satan's domain. The entire world had turned away from God in a previous earth, which led to its destruction and climatic end to all life. In Adam's world, humans had become extremely vile and again, God considered the possibility of earth's demise (Gen. 6:7).

But for one man, God would not destroy the entire earth. Noah was a just man who walked with God. God openly tested Noah's faith for all to witness. God provided Noah with a plan on how to construct a boat unlike anything previously seen on earth. Noah was instructed on what type of wood to be used, the length of the ship the width, the height, and a window on the top. Three decks were to be with rooms; and the wood was to be sealed inside and outside with pitch.

This was not easily assembled. There were no stores to order parts. Trees had to be cut to size. Each detail was handmade. The number of years required to complete the ark remains unknown. The size of the boat was approximately 625 feet long, 104 feet wide, and 62 ½ feet in height. They lived in the ark one year and seventeen days. Noah proved his faith by his sweat and labor for years despite the howling and laughter from those who refused to believe. Noah and his wife and three sons with their wives survived on the ship with the animals. All other land creatures and human beings perished beneath the waters. We are the descendants of Noah—alive, because of his faith.

Unfortunately, the ritual of animal sacrifice, even though accompanied by good works, could only extend the period of time. God ultimately deals with sin. God cannot and will not lie. "Eat from this tree and you will surely die." Sin accompanied by death is the inheritance of all Adams children. We, the children of Adam, have inherited the nature of sin. Similar to Adam we also are condemned to die.

The God Man

God's judgment was on all participants in the garden. To the serpent God said, "The seed of the woman shall crush the serpents head." In doing so, the serpent would bruise his heel (Gen. 3:15). The male contains the seed for life, not the female. Yet Isaiah the prophet referred to a birth stating, "The Lord will give you a sign. The virgin shall be with child and will give birth to a son and will call him Immanuel" (Isa. 7:14). The virgin birth was the seed of the woman, and this virgin birth was to be in a small town named Bethlehem (Micah. 5:2). Isaiah continues speaking under divine guidance stating, "For unto us a child is born, Unto us a Son is given; and the government will be upon His shoulder. His name will be called Wonderful, Counselor, Mighty God, Everlasting Father, Prince of Peace" (Isa. 9:6).

Joseph, being a just man, could not believe in a virgin birth. Then, an actual angel appeared to Joseph. The angel made known to Joseph that this was no act of man, "For that which is conceived in her is of the Holy Spirit. She will bring forth a Son, and you shall call His name Jesus, for He will save His people from their sins" (Matt. 1:18–24).

So, began the earthly ministry of the God man. He fed the hungry, healed the sick, restored sanity to the mentally insane, proclaimed good news to the poor. For this, He was despised and rejected by men. Both the Old and New Testament statements regarding Christ's appearance on earth, fit together. When a prediction is identical to the event, this would be sufficient proof in a court of law.

The Conquering Messiah

Israel is a location on earth given to Abraham and his descendants by God. Eventually, not only were the Hebrews forced to rid the land of giants, but the land has been constantly contested by others who claim legal possession of the land. Fortunately, God had promised a ruler who one day would govern the nations with authority; as it were, with a rod of iron. That day has not arrived but is definite. Daniel had prophesied of such a visitation to earth and it's time and location has yet to be determined (Dan. 9:20–27).

What some have failed to recognize is that this strong man would come to earth on two separate occasions. His first appearance is in human flesh and bones, the helpless infant, the lamb of God as a sin offering. As the angel had said, "He will save His people from their sins."

God becoming man is heaven's most valued gift to humanity. It's nice that we exist, but if we must suffer in the after-life without a recourse, what then? Jesus said of Judas, "It would had been good for Judas, had he never been born (Mk. 14). The Bible tells us, "It is appointed unto men once to die, but after this the judgment" (Heb. 9:27).

Christ in the Old Testament

The Old Testament account of Christ as told by the prophets contains details that are not included in the New Testament. The prophets were able to see what occurred behind closed doors. In the New Testament, they were limited to what was reported or seen.

The word of the Lord came to Micah. "But you, Bethlehem Ephrathah, though you are little among the thousands of Judah, yet out of you shall come forth to Me the One to be Ruler in Israel, whose going forth are from of old, from everlasting. In Micah 5:2, Zechariah declared,

"Behold, your king is coming to you; He is just
and having salvation, holy and riding on a donkey,
a colt, the foal of a donkey." (Zech. 9:9–10, Matt. 21:2–11)

Daniel in a vision saw Him, "One like the Son of Man, coming with the clouds of heaven" (Dan. 1:13–14).

In Psalms, we read God's message to His son: "You are My Son, today I have begotten you. Ask of me, and I will give you the nations for your inheritance, and the ends of the earth for your possession. You shall slash them to pieces like a potter's vessel" (Psalms 2:7–9).

The Man Jesus

For the duration of approximately four thousand years, animal sacrifice and rigorous obligations were observed in the hope for eternal life. It had been revealed to Daniel that Jerusalem would be rebuilt. God would send the anointed One, a ruler, one who would rule the earth with a rod of iron. Such a qualified leader was desperately needed. One who would bring pride to the nation. He would be ranked among the noblemen, a monarch respected by all.

But what came? A crying infant that soiled it's clothing. A child born out of wedlock, and Joseph who claimed not to be the child's father. A wood worker might he be, not a ruler having the ability to govern the world.

This Jesus claimed to be neither a Jew nor a gentile from Joseph's side of the family. But claims maternal inheritance from Mary's side. Mary is an offspring, a descendent to King David. As stated by God in Eden's garden, that one day, a woman would give birth to a male child without the aid from any male. This seed would be "the seed of the woman" (Gen. 3:15).

Jesus was despised even while in his mother's womb. The prophet Isaiah wrote regarding Christs coming to earth, that He would be despised and rejected by men (Isa. 53:3).

While many births are celebrated, King Herod became frightened that this Jesus would one day dethrone him. As a result, King Herod ordered that all the male children two years and younger in Bethlehem and the surrounding land, be put to death.

Jeremiah heard the weeping, six hundred years before Christ's birth and wrote, "A voice was heard in Ramah, Lamentation, and bitter weeping; Rachel weeping for her children refused to be comforted for her children were no more" (Jer. 31:15).

Thirty years quietly passed, as the child became a man. The following three years would complete the purpose for Christ's existence as a human on earth. In those three years, Jesus revealed his true identity. He healed those who were sick, restored life to the dead, fed thousands of people from a hand full of food, walked on the water, and when the weather became a dangerous storm, Jesus told the wind to cease. Instantly the weather became peaceful.

Despite God's peace on earth, the threat to the organized religious world was met with angered violence. The sudden fear of the new born King caused King Herod to panic and this also possessed organized religion.

The Arrest

A very joyous holiday was in progress. The feast of unleavened bread, the Passover. A detachment of Roman soldiers were on duty to maintain order at the festival. These armed cohorts also assisted the priests in the apprehending of a dangerous individual who likely would be protected by a band of like-minded individuals. Both Matthew and Mark reported that the priests were accompanied by a great multitude with swords. The gospels inform us that these armed individuals were the Roman military (Matt. 27:27; Lk. 23:11, 3, 6; John 19:2).

The Pharisee priesthood and the Levites desired to rid the world from this man Jesus. The problem was that Jesus had thousands of followers. Therefore, the priests had their hands tied, unable to touch Jesus in any legal manor. Then Judas came to the rescue.

It was high moon in an olive grove named Gethsemane. A garden where Jesus often rested from the demands of the many people. Judas, being one of the twelve disciples, knew where the Lord would be. For thirty pieces of silver, Judas led the convoy to the location where Jesus rested. Five hundred years earlier, Zechariah wrote, "So they weighed out for my wages thirty pieces of silver" (Zech. 11:12).

The Roman soldiers had no idea as to who Jesus was. The priests would rather not be the ones who point out Jesus. So, it fell on Judas to provide a sign as to which of the men Jesus was. "Whoever I kiss, He is the One; Seize Him" (Matt. 26:48).

Then, Judas led the detachment of troops, which included officers from the chief priest to the garden. There waiting for them stood Jesus who asked, "Who are you looking for?" Judas remained quiet, but those in the military answered, "Jesus of Nazareth." Jesus answered, "I am He." The moment Jesus spoke, it was as if God stood there and the volume of His voice caused the soldiers to topple, not forward, but backward. They collapsed to the ground as dead men (John 18:6).

As they stood to their feet, all fighting had vanished. The unseen power that had sent them to the ground was far superior than was the Roman military. For the second time, Jesus asked, "Whom are you seeking?" With reluctance, they replied, "Jesus of Nazareth." In somewhat of an insulting manner Jesus answered, "I have told you, I am He."

Two years earlier, Jesus angered the people. They had become so angry that they wanted to kill Jesus. Jesus simply walked through the raging crowd who were unable to apprehend Him (Lk. 4:30). Now as before, no one could lay their hand on Jesus without His permission. Peter leaped forward, swung his sword at the high priest's servants heads but missed; instead cut off his right ear of one of the servants. Jesus simply told Peter, not to do that Jesus then, picked up the ear from the ground and placed it onto the wound and immediately, it was though it had never happened.

Had the armed soldiers been in charge, Peter would have been butchered on the spot because of his act. The priests and the Roman garrisons were not in charge. Jesus was not a captive. He surrendered His body as a sacrifice for many. God in Jesus were the ones in charge. Now in the act of full surrender, Jesus was delivered to the office of the high priest. It was the high priest who would personally see to it that Jesus would have a fair trial.

The Suffering Messiah

Strange as to why some people hate the true light. Truth and reality is the light that reveals the mischief that is hid under a cover of darkness. Those who shine light will be criticized, even hated by those who prefer darkness rather than light. Jesus said, "I am the light of the world" (Jn. 8:12). As a result, Jesus was hated even by the clergy.

Jesus immediately was taken into the high priest's chambers where the inquiry and acquisitions began. This was not a matter that could be left for tomorrow. This demanded immediate action. This Jesus must pay for His horrendous crimes.

Christ's arrest suddenly became known throughout Jerusalem and the courtyard soon filled with very angry religious people. Angry they are, because of Jesus claim and His followers professing a new religion. The inquiry demanded answers, a confession from Jesus that He was guilty of teaching myths rather than truth. Stern slaps developed into fists on the cheeks of Jesus, yet He said nothing.

Early in the morning, the elders of the people, the chief priests, and the Scribes, led Him to their council hall. Again, the inquiry continued. "If you are really the Christ, tell us?"

"Are you really God's son?"

Jesus answered, "You rightly say that I am." With those words, the multitude led Jesus to Pilate, accusing Him of perverting the nation, not paying taxes, and claiming to be a King!

After Pilates's interrogation of Jesus, Pilate announced, "I find no fault in the man."

Pilates words so outraged the Israelite leaders that Pilate had to make a concession. He would send Jesus to be examined by King Herod. If the King was willing to hear the case, this would be a high honor to all.

When King Herod saw Jesus, he was exceedingly glad and desired to see miracles. King Herod questioned Jesus in a lengthy session, without Jesus replying to a single word. While, the priests and Scribes who accompanied Jesus, vehemently accused Him. King Herod found this silent behavior insulting. King Herod, the world's most feared king was humiliated in the presence of the chief priest, Scribes, and officers of the military. In retaliation, Jesus was treated with contempt and mocked once again. Jesus was dressed as a king then was stripped of His clothing and returned to Pontius Pilate.

Neither Pilate nor King Herod was able to find fault in Jesus (Lk. 23:14–15). The priest's power to dominate over the people was threatened and to infer that these good people should repent from sin, was an insult that had gone too far. Pilate, desiring to release Jesus, also hoped to please his people. Rather than crucifying Jesus as the people demanded, Pilate surrendered Jesus to the tormenters, thinking that this would appease the people (Lk. 23:16).

When Jesus gave away free food, thousands of people came for the fest. Facing death, Jesus stood alone. Where were the blind that now could see, the crippled who could now walk: Good people hid or denied knowing of Jesus even as Peter had denied the Christ Jesus.

At this time in history, Rome exhibited extreme cruelty to non-Roman criminals. Remains of the Colosseum still exist in which thousands of people gathered weekly to be entertained by the death of others. The hall where Jesus was sent was operated by men who achieved pleasure in the suffering of others.

Before flogging began, the masters of cruelty desired to enjoy the presents of the famous king. Everything a person wanted to do to someone better than themselves, this was their opportunity. They striped Him naked. Struck Him with their fists and slapped Him. The soldiers' cruel behavior was such that each of them, attempted to outdo one another. A scarlet robe was placed on Him. Another formed a crown using branches from a thorn bush and placed it on His head. A slap, using the flat side of the sword on the crown, caused the inch-long thorns to prick the scalp, causing pain as the blood ran down the face of Jesus. "Hail, King of the Jews!" said the Roman guards, as they spit, slapped and pulled on Jesus's beard. When they became fatigued with their torturous behavior, it was time for the flogging to climax the excitement.

The flogging was performed using a leather strap attached to a wood handle. The leather strap contained bits of sharp iron or bone fragments. Each lash cut into the victim's flesh. The naked victim had his hands tied to a low post, causing a bent over position. His sex glans were fully exposed. Flogging cause the death of many people.

To understand the full depth of what transpired behind closed doors, we retreat to the ancient prophets who by divine revelation, revealed the life and death of Jesus. Hundreds even thousands of years prior to His advent.

In 712 BC, Isaiah described the words and thoughts of the suffering Messiah. Jesus would come to the earth on two separate occasions. The first arrival would be a helpless infant. Human, yet perfect without sin in order to be the sacrificial lamb of God. Jesus would suffer all the pains of humanity and die bearing the sins of the entire world. His second coming will be as the conquering Messiah. He then will rule over the entire earth in a manner of speaking as with a rod of iron. We hear the suffering of Jesus through the voice of Isaiah:

> "I was not rebellious, nor did I turn away.
> I gave My back to those who struck Me,
> and My cheeks to those who plucked out
> the beard; I did not hide My face from shame
> and spitting." (Isa. 50:5–6)

According to the life and works of Flavius Josephus, Jesus was whipped until his bones were laid bare (pg. 825). In addition to the flogging was the fists, slaps, and spitting on Jesus's face. They also "plucked out His beard." To pull out a fully developed beard as Jesus had required more than one person. His body had to hold in place as others pulled on the beard. This was not one hair thread at a time. This was a hand full of hair at once. For a full beard to be plucked from the face of a male, would also pull flesh attached to the beard. This on-slot of torture by the young Romans soldiers would have scarred Jesus so that He would have become unrecognizable to many. Isaiah wrote:

> "His visage was marred more than any
> man, His form more than the sons of men."
> (Isa. 52:14)

In His suffering, Jesus again proved His deity. In the words spoken by the Prophet Isaiah, no human has ever survived such torture as would Jesus. Our world is both physical and unseen. We are both physical and spiritual and to be successful, both the physical and spiritual must be addressed. The unseen world is very active, and we are the focus of unseen forces. It was evil spirits that inspired hatred toward Jesus. An unseen force that is relentless in its denial of truth and exists today. The Prophet asks the question to us. "Who has believed our report?" (Isaiah 53:1).

And to whom is this branch (Jesus) of God been revealed? (Isaiah 53:2). From birth, He shall grow up as a tender plant. He has no special features. His appearance is common (Isaiah 53:3). Despite a normal childhood, in His adult years, He stood apart from those His own age; a little distant as reserved for a particular purpose. He became despised and rejected, people avoided contact with Him. He became acquainted with loneliness and grief (Isaiah 53:4). God placed on Jesus all the sorrows, pains, and afflictions known to mankind (Isaiah 53:5). Why? He was wounded for our transgressions. He was bruised for our iniquities. The chastisement for our peace was upon Him, and by His stripes we are healed (Isaiah 53:6). All have sinned; each has gone their own way. Regardless of how extreme our sin, it was placed on Jesus (Isaiah 53:7). Despite that He had committed no wrong, He opened not His mouth. He died so that we may live (Isaiah 53:8). On the cross, Jesus with a loud voice said, "It is finished." Then gave up the ghost. However, it was not over. Jesus died a sinners' death. All the sins of the world were on Jesus. Because of the sin, Jesus descended into the lower regions of the earth. Into Hell, He descended.

One thousand years before Christ's advent to earth, the Psalms revealed what became of Christ. Immediately upon His death, Jesus speaking to His Father God said, you will not leave my soul in Hell, neither will you allow your Holy One to see corruption (Psalm 16:10). Only deity can be referred to as the "Holy One." These identical words are repeated in the New Testament, after Christ's death and His resurrection.

> "You will not leave my soul in hell, neither
> will you suffer your Holy One to see
> corruption." (Acts 2:27, 31)

Isaiah 53:8 states, "He was taken from prison and from judgment." Hell, nor the grave could hold Him. He had committed no violence neither was there any deceit in His mouth (Isaiah 53:10). It pleased God to bruise Him because He (Jesus) was made an offering for sin (Isaiah 53:11). Because the sins of the world were placed on Christ, "many shall be justified."

A New Doctrine!

In the days of Jesus, all scripture existed on rolls of parchment paper that were written by Moses and other prophets. These were regarded as containing the very voice of God. Jesus and His disciples spoke exclusively from these scrolls that predicted the coming of Jesus. These scrolls contained the actual eye witnesses and accounts of what was to be said and transpired in the past hundreds even thousands of years, at the time of Christ. New witnesses began to appear. John the Baptist as was the Christ himself and others, were essential caricatures referred to in the Old Testament scrolls.

The birth of Jesus introduced the greatest gift to humanity equal in value as was the creation itself. If we were doomed to suffering without a savior, it would have been preferred that we not exist. Jesus was the fulfillment to many scriptures as described by the prophets. One such chapter is the book of Psalms chapter 22, where David became the voice of the suffering messiah.

In order for the Old Testament saints to have hope to achieve heaven, there were a list of obligations legally binding on each person. Emotions were personal and obedience to the law was essential. Without conforming to the law, this could result in death by stoning. As years drifted by, new laws were adopted, and religion frequently became a business rather than serving God.

The prophets never changed. They had a contact with God that was different than most other people. John the Baptist was a prophet (Matt. 11:7–11). Jesus was more than a prophet. He presented a doctrine that was new to people who already were religious. The people thought they knew all the answers.

For more than four thousand years, humans had observed and were compliant in keeping the laws and rites as prescribed to them. Then, this man named Jesus, came and expected people to believe that ceremonies do not provide a way to heaven! What will He say next? That possibly He will replace the death of lambs?

The practice to obey rules and regulations is within the ability of all humans. Despite our good works and human suffering, heaven is no guarantee. The New Testament message is to be filled with God's Holy Spirit through repentance (Acts 3:19). When we do our part, God will do His. "As many as received Him, to them gave He power to become the sons of God" (John 1:12).

The prophets had a contact with God that was foreign to the normal church attendee as were many of their priests. The New Testament reveals a life that mimics the spirit life of the prophets. By the use of God's word, all true Christians become a prophet at times.

Jesus revealed the key to eternal life by telling a true story. A devout Jewish ruler named Nicodemus, hoping not to be recognized, came to Jesus in the night. Nicodemus said, "Rabbi, we know you are a teacher sent from God because, no man would be able to do these miracles except, God."

Recognizing the sincerity of Nicodemus, Jesus replied, "I will tell you the truth. Except a man be born again, he will never enter God's Kingdom." This statement left Nicodemus speechless. Who had ever heard such nonsense? Was an old man going to re-enter his mothers' womb to be born a second time?

Then, Jesus repeated His statement adding, "This was not a physical birth, rather a spiritual birth" (Jn. 3:1–6, Acts 13:10). Previously we inherited the nature of sin from our parents, Adam and Eve. We had no say in the matter. Jesus represented a new day in which we are invited to change our birth certificate from a sinner to a saint.

Because of the sin of one man, sin and death was passed onto each human. In a similar manor, the death of one "just" man, took my place in death. I was the sinner, not He, Christ, took my place in death. All have sinned, and as a result, we are all doomed, destined for death. Because we all are sinful, Christ was sent from heaven to become the sacrifice for the world. My sin was placed on Christ. In death, bearing the sins of the world, Christ descended into the depths of the earth, into a fire burning with brimstone (Rev. 14:10). However, this was an injustice, Christ had committed no sin and hell was unable to hold Him. Because of one man, Adam, all humans became sinful and guilty. Because of the death of one righteous man, sin is commuted through faith in Jesus Christ (Rom. 5:12–19).

Jesus hung on the cross between two convicted criminals. One of the convicts angrily ridiculed Jesus saying, "If you are God's son, why don't you get yourself down and take us with you? The other thief replied, 'Have you no fear of God? We are guilty of our crimes, but this man had committed no crime.' Then the thief requested; 'Lord, remember me when you enter your Kingdom.' Jesus replied, 'Today you will be with me in paradise'" (Lk. 23:39–43).

What some consider as essential had no value to the thief. The thief acknowledged his guilt and asked Jesus to remember him. He died and woke up in paradise. The other thief died and woke up in hell. Water baptism is good but saves no one. Good works has a reward but saves no one. Both sinner and saint suffer, but to suffer fails to open Heavens door. The door to Heaven is through Jesus.

Only Jesus could provide the sin offering acceptable to the Father, due to the fact that Jesus had no sin. The proof of Jesus perfection was the fact of His resurrection from the dead. Jesus was the only perfect sin offering given on behalf of humankind. Jesus is the door through whom we must pass, the only entry into heaven (John 14:6). All other suggestions are false hopes.

> "For God so loved the world, that He gave His
> only son, that whosoever believeth in Him should
> not perish, but have everlasting life." (John 3:16)

Chapter 7

✳ ✳ ✳ ✳ ✳

From Here to Eternity

The prophet Jeremiah called for the people to repent of their ways. The people obeyed the voice of false prophets. Religious hypocrisy was a thriving enterprise. The people had become totally unfaithful, without integrity, even the courts and rulers became dishonest. Jeremiah warned that destruction would come suddenly. Then Jeremiah, under inspired utterance, recounted details of an earlier earth having great cities filled with people and creatures of enormous stature that abruptly ended due to a steady increase in wicked deeds and disrespect for their Creator. This first world vanished, never to live again (Jer. 4:23–26).

A New Earth

After a long sleep, earth awoke to the sound of God's voice. "Let there be light" and light appeared. When all arrangements were completed, Eve made her appearance. But hiding in the bush was that old heckler Lucifer, who caused all the problems during the first world.

Some 1,650 years drifted by and earth again became a habitat for great evil, to the extent that nature was altered, causing an epidemic of giant beings, both human and giant animals (Gen. 6:4–5). It was at that time in history that a civilized people became brutal without regard for others, to the point of no return. This caused God to unleash judgment on the earth again in the form of a flood.

During Noah's flood, eight humans survived in addition to a male and female of each species of earth's creatures. Jeremiah informs us that the first world had been totally eliminated with no exceptions (Jer. 4:23–26). In Noah's flood, life survived.

God's Covenant

Some two thousand years had elapsed since Adam had walked with God and again the world had forgotten their Creator. Man, a free-thinking being, decided he had no need of a God. Man decided to be his own god and chose to form a divinity of his own choosing. Humanity preferred a dumb object to worship that could neither hear nor speak.

There was a man named Abram whose father Terah led his family in the worship of idols. For some unknown reason, God made known to Abram that He, God, was real. Eventually Abram became Abraham, who married a woman named Sarai.

Abraham became very wealthy, having many employees. One such person was a maid named Hagar, who bore Abraham a son whose name was Ishmael. God blessed Ishmael, stating that he would become a great nation. This became true. God then made a covenant with Abraham and a promise that Sarai would bear him a son whose name was to be Isaac. The covenant given Abraham would be established with Isaac as an everlasting covenant with Isaac's descendants (Gen. 17:19–21).

This covenant agreed to between God and Abraham became very restrictive in the days of Moses. To obey God's rule would bring good health, prosperity, protection from violence in the streets, from other nations, and from the sky. To dishonor God would result in the very opposite. You will suffer disease, enemies will defeat you, and you will be scattered among the nations (Leviticus 26).

It was only a small minority of Isaac's descendants who adhered to each detail of the Mosaic laws—a trend that still exists for both Jew and Gentile. Most people adhere to a limited practice of faith that will not alter their lifestyle!

Malachi is the final book in the Old Testament written by a prophet who becomes the voice of God to the people. The Jews survived seventy years of captivity under the Persian Empire, which came to an abrupt end due to Alexander the Great. The Israelis dispersed to numerous nations, some to Jerusalem, some stayed in Persia, others settled in Egypt and elsewhere. Despite living in many nations, a mystical union binds them together as a nation within many nations. Their home is Israel; elsewhere, they are pilgrims on a journey.

Just prior to the dispersing of Israel as a nation, Malachi delivered a final message. God had judged the people because of their failure of obedience. Despite their awareness of what is right or wrong, they chose to do what is wrong. Four hundred years would pass without a prophet, without utterance from God. Palestine would remain under the thumb of foreign nations. The Mac Cabeans heroically fought to regain Jewish sovereignty but came to a sudden halt when the Roman Empire stepped on Palestine.

Out from the darkness of a religious night came John the Baptist crying for the people to repent, to prepare for the Lord's appearance. It was a new day not only for Israel but for the entire world.

By 70 AD, Rome had completely destroyed Jerusalem. Those who survived attempted to find refuge in many nations.

Two thousand years would pass as the empty land baked in the sun. There were no forests, no rain; the desert claimed the wasteland as its own.

In 1948, the United Nations established a ruling that the desert once occupied by the Israelites would be officially named as the "State of Israel." A trickle of Israelites began to leave their adopted countries for the promised land once again. By the end of the twentieth century, the nation flourished with cities, towns, and harvests of such abundance that they now export goods on the world market. Because the Hebrew people broke their backs to restore the land, turning a desert into a flowering rose, outsiders who gave nothing except complaints would now like to have possession of the land.

The Great Tribulation (Matt. 24)

The disciples inquired of Jesus, "What will be the sign of your return to earth and the end of the age?" Jesus replied that religious apostasy would become common, deceiving many. Those who have durable faith in Jehovah will face persecution and possible death. Real faith in Christ will be despised—false deities will be embraced. Those on earth will suffer wars and rumors of wars, famine, and multiple earthquakes. The earth will be bombarded by objects from the sky. There will be great distress on the earth unequaled from the beginning of the world until then, and never to be equaled again. If those days had not been shortened, no one would survive. These are the words of the Lord.

Prediction versus Prophecy

To predict is the human ability to state opinions as to what may occur at a later date. Prophecy is not an act of human ability. The prophet is a person who speaks for God under divine guidance and is never wrong. Many claims to speak for God or to be God's prophet. If their word is untrue or their claim is proven false, this person is a hoax and not to be believed.

The Man John

John, a hardened fisherman by trade, became a devoted follower of Christ, the "beloved disciple." Religion controlled all the affairs in Jerusalem including, medication and the law. Sin could only be forgiven by a priest who offered a sacrifice on their behalf to God. The sacrifice could be purchased for a price on church property then offered to God in the same location. This angered Jesus (Lk. 19:45). Religion had become a profitable business. The clergy was expected to manifest proper behavior. To the contrary, they were liars, stole from the public, and were willing to murder to protect their sovereignty.

During the crucifixion, Mary stood weeping by the feet of Jesus. The disciples were hiding in fear for their lives except for John. John defiantly stood by Mary's side in full view of the Roman guard. John wrote three of the gospels in which the last two he referred to himself as the elder. Age being a standard for dignity and wisdom in his day.

All the disciples came to untimely deaths, not because of wrongdoing, but because of their testimony of Christ rather than to adopt a secular version of religious tolerance. The one exception of longevity was John who for unknown reasons was not assassinated. Instead, John, near the age of ninety, was banished on an island known as Patmos. Patmos was off the coast of Asia, a land mass six miles wide by ten miles long. Without hotels, restaurants, or stores, John was abandoned to manage his own final days.

He had witnessed the death of all his friends, even Jesus. John believed that Jesus was to be the Messiah who would deliver the people. Now all had evaporated, gone, nothing was left but to die and he would do so alone. Only the seagulls would witness his final end. As he sat on the earth accepting his fate, a voice spoke having the strength and velocity of a trumpet. Startled, John turned to see this voice when instantly John entered the unseen world of the future. There he witnessed the demise of the earth and saw a new heaven and a new earth, a spectacle that was beyond all the accumulated events of his life. This became John's finest hour.

John's revelation began with a warning to the people and their churches. The church is a reflection, a spiritual thermometer of man's standing with God. Humans are the church and a church without the voice of God is a worthless practice.

John's revelation stated that the church lost its first love, becoming cold and spiritually empty, a reflection of modern culture. In the last days, there will be a sharp increase in religious philosophies dealing with all aspects of human behavior. Prophets, teachers of every persuasion will offer their goods on the open market while rejecting the true light.

False religion will continue throughout the tribulation. In fact, many will claim to be Christ or to know where He could be located. During those years, prosecution of true believers will be constant.

This includes the Hebrew people due to the fact that Judaism and Christianity came from the same source. The Christian can denounce his faith and in so doing can be spared from prosecution or possible death. Few Jews are avowed followers of Judaism, yet that does not minimize their blame for Christianity. When Christians suffer, the Jews will also suffer.

Some of these false teachers will be so persuasive that many will turn away from their faith for a lie (Matt. 24:11–13, 24). Those who are unwilling to live in accordance to their faith will also be unwilling to die for their faith. Jesus said, "Those who endure to the end, the same shall be saved" (Matt. 24:13).

The indifference to Christian principles is the first sign of the coming judgment. "The love of many shall become cold" (Matt. 24:12). Hatred, anger, and jealousy have affected people and nations, causing wars and the rumors of wars. Violence occurring in the streets, sexual depravity, and dishonest behavior has become the normal, even in children. At the time of birth, if the doctor is no longer able to identify whether it's a male or female—it's time for correction. The same mental disorder that caused the destruction of the first world, and again in Noah's day has again invaded our modern civilization.

The pill has destroyed marriage. Intimate relations strictly for sport have replaced the sacredness of marriage. The home is in shambles and as a result the children have gone wild.

This is why, in creation, the home is one of God's most sacred institutions. In biblical terms, the home is a type of Christ and His church; we the people, are the body and bride of Christ, "in a spiritual manner of speaking." As the home goes, so goes the nation.

Harry S. Truman, thirty-second president of the United States said, "If you want a friend, get a dog." Dogs that have learned obedience can be man's best friend. Unsupervised, dogs in the wild or in packs are a danger to children and other animals.

The home is a child's first institute in a long process of learning. The absence of a mother or a father hampers children in their development of lifelong skills achieved by parents. Proper training of a child from home is the most substantial education available at any price. Proper discipline absent during childhood has led to a culture of delinquent minors, who rebel at all forms of control. Children who have been properly tutored have respect for those in authority. The need for police in schools, streets that are unsafe to walk on, reveals a people who have lost their way.

Knowledge Shall Increase (Daniel 12:4)

Man has been on earth how many years? The anatomy of the human brain has not increased nor decreased over thousands of years. Ancient writings have all the logic and reasoning of modern literature. This indicates an identical anatomy of the brain.

Horse-drawn carriages have provided transportation many thousands of years. This has remained true until the late eighteenth century. Suddenly a transfiguration occurred in the nineteenth century so dramatic that the eighteenth century had little resemblance to the nineteenth and twentieth centuries. Horses no longer work the streets, phones existed without wires, the preferred method of long distance travel is through the air, and man has walked on the moon.

The human brain had not changed even while knowledge had suddenly risen to astonishing heights. What happened? Some three thousand years earlier, God said that just prior to the end of days "knowledge shall be increased" (Dan. 12:4).

The final seven years of the coming judgment will be unlike any previous encounter on earth. The elimination of life will be so extensive that in the final end, for a human to locate another live person would be as rare as to find pure gold (Isa. 13:6–13) Jesus had said, "Unless those days were shortened, no life would survive (Matt. 24:22, Mk. 13:20).

Storms are preceded by warnings. The sky darkens, the wind howls, thunder is heard in the distance. Today warning lights and sounds are flashing, forecasting in advance the destruction that is about to occur.

The Last Rumble

With moral behavior in decline, spiritual blindness will infect even those thought to be religious (Matt. 24:12). Peace will vanish, replaced with violence (Rev. 6:4). Cruel behavior, poverty, and famine will become epidemic (Rev. 6:6–8). Oppression of the righteous and attempts to kill them will become common (Rev. 6:91). War between nations and starvation will become dominant over a fourth part of the earth (Rev. 6:8). Slaughter of the righteous will be massive. John saw those who were killed because of their faith pleading with God: "How long will You allow Your people to be massacred? When will You avenge the guilty because of our blood?" (Rev. 6:8–11).

This wicked behavior against God will result in a major earthquake and affect the sky above. The sun will become black, the moon as blood; the stars will fall from the sky, earth will shake with such violence that mountains will be moved from their location, and islands in the sea will vanish (Rev. 6:12–14).

John's vision of stars falling from the sky may appear as fiction today. Two thousand years ago, John believed the stars to exist as he saw them—tiny shining specks in the sky. John had no idea of their size nor distance. As specks of dust or solid particles penetrate earth's atmosphere, their speed causes such heat that the meteor particle becomes vaporized. What John believed to be stars in reality were flaming meteors.

Events of that hour will cause total panic worldwide. Whether rich or poor, king or ruler, all will believe that the end of the world had come and that the living God was angry with them (Rev. 6:15–17). Some will repent; the majority does not. This is followed by a great slaughter of God's people.

When the righteous go to heaven, they are clothed with white robes in preparation to stand before God's throne. In this scene of heaven, a multitude of saints were assassinated during the great tribulation and are now dressed with clean white robes, never again to die, hunger or thirst, nor depend on the sun's light (Rev. 7:9–17).

Horror suddenly filled the sky with voices of thunder—lightning that turned the black sky into day and fire fell from the sky. The earth trembled, as blood-colored hail fell to the ground, and flaming particles rained on other parts of the earth killing a third of all earth's vegetation (Rev. 8:5–7). Burning meteoroids raining on the earth would not be limited to vegetation but also would include structures such as buildings, homes, human life, automobiles, factories, oil wells, or any object beneath such a torrent of destruction.

As if that was not enough, a large burning comet or asteroid, said to be the size of a mountain, will slam into one of the oceans. A third of the sea creatures will die, and a third of the ships in the sea will be destroyed (Rev. 8:8–9). A wave of water caused by such an event would eliminate every structure within miles of the seacoast as though they had never existed.

A second large object will fall on the land, polluting one third of earth's fresh water supply. The pollution contains a live toxin named wormwood, which will result in the death of many who unknowingly drink the water (Rev. 8:10–11). This will be followed by the darkening of the sun and moon. The sun will only provide its light for a third of a normal day, and the moon and stars will be visible for a third of the night (Rev. 8:12).

John then saw what he believed to be a star fall from the sky and hit the earth with such force that it formed a pit having such depth that smoke equal to a volcano darkened the sun (Rev. 9:1).

In the Gulf of Mexico exists a large cavity in earth's crust believed to have occurred 65 million years ago. The crater remains 125 miles wide and ten miles deep. It is believed to have been formed by a comet six miles wide and traveling at eighteen miles per second. The results may have caused acid rain, global wildfires, and blocked the sun's light, causing a prolonged winter lasting many thousands of years. This event is believed by many to have caused the extinction of the dinosaurs.

John saw the smoke from the falling star, so dense and dark that the smoke literally had to have escaped from hell. The smoke further restricted the sun's light. Out from the smoke came a new plague, strange locusts that are nonvegetarian; they are carnivores. Though their size is similar to locusts, their body resembles a horse having a human face and a woman's long hair. Their teeth are very distinctive and sharp. In flight, their wings create the sound of galloping horses. Their purpose is to torment humans with a bite that causes such pain that a victim desires to die. Five months they will torment the human race (Rev. 9:3–11).

Peter refers to angels so wicked that God had to confine them to hell (2 Pet 2:4). Some of those same angels (demons/devils) will be released for short time. While free on earth, they kill one-third of the remaining human race by the use of smoke, fire, and brimstone (Rev. 9:14–19). Despite all the plagues, people will not call on God nor show Him any respect. They continued in the worship of devils, sorceries, commit fornication, murder, and robberies (Rev. 9:20–21). Due to man's rejection of their Creator, man's sorrows continue.

God will send two preachers with the gospel message to Jerusalem. They will preach in the streets, in every corner where people gathered, urging them to turn from doing what was wrong. A very large number of the city's people had become totally corrupt, equal to that of Sodom and Gomorrah. All the city's people will hear the message; many will hate the message and the messengers. The people will be tormented by the message, but refusing to change their behavior. They will be willing to dispose of the problem by killing the two preachers and leave their bodies in the street as a memorial to their success. With glee, the people celebrated the deaths of the preachers and while the festival continues, a severe earthquake strikes the city. A tenth part of Jerusalem will fall, killing seven thousand people (Rev. 11:2–13).

The Final Three and a Half Years

The great Roman Empire that once dominated the world will attempt to rise again. As King Nebuchadnezzar slept, God gave him a dream. In the dream, he saw nations that would dominate the world, beginning from his day to the second coming of Christ to earth (Daniel 2).

Nebuchadnezzar was the head of gold, represented by the Neo-Babylonian Empire in 605–539 BC. This was followed by the Medo-Persian empire established by Cyrus in 539 BC. The third empire was established by Alexander the Great in 330 BC. The fourth king-dom was strong as iron. The Roman Empire began about 67 BC and dominated over a thousand years. The stone that broke to pieces all of earth's kingdoms is the second coming of Christ, who is to rule over the entire earth for a thousand years.

Rome was represented by the legs of iron; the feet will form near or during the tribulation. The feet will be a mix of iron and clay. Iron for strength, and clay is easily broken. The ten toes represent ten nations that form an alliance. These nations once formed the great Roman Empire, but now not as strong because of the clay. The orig-inal empire was under the rule of a single entity. In the new alliance, each nation is sovereign which forms the clay. Three of those nations will break their agreement—leaving an alliance of seven.

While the ten nations exist, a strong leader will rise out from them having such influence that his strength dominates over the world. He is able to dominate the alliance so that his military estab-lishment distinguishes him from all other nations. He will demon-strate his military superior strength shortly after arriving on the national stage by eliminating one of the ten nations in the alliance.

He will be known as the beast, the antichrist, and by his num-ber, which is 666. He hates God, hates all who believe in God and hates the Jewish people. He openly blasphemes the God of heaven and claims that he is God and is to be worshiped. He will be given spiritual powers so that he is able to perform acts beyond human limitations; many people will be deceived.

The beast then orders a decree, "All that dwell on the earth must worship him" (Rev. 13:8). To prove that a person worships the beast, his number, 666 must be placed on the right hand or on their fore-head. Without the mark, no one can buy food nor sell without the number. Anyone without the number is to be killed (Rev. 13:15–18). Warning: Those who receive his mark will not be allowed entrance into heaven (Rev. 14:9–11).

"All that dwell upon the earth shall worship him" (Rev. 13:8). The people will say, "Who is like unto the beast? Who is able to make war with him?" (Rev. 13:4). It's in this critical hour that the gospel will be preached to every nation, kindred, and tongue, throughout the entire world (Rev. 14:6–7). The devil will empower the beast with the will and strength to kill saints (Rev. 13:7). Those who choose to live may do so by worshiping the beast. Those who die for their testimony of Christ can rejoice—for in heaven they will live again forever (Rev. 12:11–12). The slaughter of God's people will be huge (Rev. 14:3–7, 15:2–4). In return, they will live again. Those who embrace the beast one day will die. Standing before God, they will be condemned to the lake of fire (Rev. 20:12–15).

The Great Whore (Rev. 17)

A second major religion will be in existence at the time of the beast and as belligerent—willing to kill those who oppose her. She is called a whore because she pretends to be the true path that leads to heaven. She is not the way to heaven, neither is she related to the true God. She is a deceiver concealing her true identity, a devil in disguise. Similar to the beast, she hates Jehovah and those who follow Him. Her history began in earnest approximately 77 AD with roots that extend much earlier. The goddess Isis, having statues, temples, and priests, existed before Christ's birth (Antiquities of the Jews Josephus, pg. 536). On this woman's forehead are the words "Babylon the Great" and "she was drunk with the blood of the saints" (Rev. 17:5–6). Babylon, the ancient city on the lower Euphrates River, is now central Iraq, noted for wealth, luxury, and wickedness in ancient times.

Both the whore and the beast demand to be worshiped. For this reason, the beast hates the woman (Rev. 17:16–17). In one day, the beast totally eliminates the whore's power. Today, we see this woman's influence rapidly attempting to control the entire world and, to a large extent, she will succeed. We know this because, with her demise, there is worldwide weeping and great sorrow because of her demise (Rev. 18:2–24).

Those who worship the prostitute would also worship the beast for convenience. Several plagues affect only those who are marked with the beast's number, such as the locust plague (9:3–10) and a grievous unidentified sore (Rev. 16:2).

All earth's oceans except for one has escaped judgment. A plague sweeps across each ocean, turning its water into a likeness of blood. The contamination kills every living object in the seas. The great fresh water bodies including rivers and springs turn into the likeness of blood (Rev. 16:3–4).

Solar flares facing earth explode causing such heat that humans become scorched as if they had been in a fire. The great river Euphrates completely dries up. People gnawed their tongues in pain, cursing the God of heaven. Rather than asking for God's mercy, they blasphemed the only One who had power to end the plagues. These people know God exists, but their hate causes them to curse the One who created them (Rev. 16:8–12)

Armageddon

All the world will worship the beast except for three groups:

1. Christians will not worship the beast.
2. The prostitute demands worship for herself.
3. The Jews have gathered to their own land from the nations of the world.

The beast, possessed by the devil, hates the Jew and Christians above all others (Rev. 12:13). He is determined not just to kill the Jew, but to blot out the memory of their existence.

The beast's military can easily demolish Israel. But for unknown reasons plots a scheme to involve all the nations on earth to join him in the assault against the Hebrews. He will eliminate the Jewish problem forever!

After many days, armies representing the nations of the world will gather on the location in northern Israel. A plain that extends from the Jordan River valley to a coastal plain near Mt. Carmel, a distance of nearly two hundred miles. This empty flat waste land in the Hebrew language was named "Armageddon."

The world had drastically changed in just a few years. Aircraft are no longer an option due to the violence in the atmosphere.

Runways are in shambles due to the numerous earthquakes. Oil rigs and the mechanics for the production of fuel lay in ruin. Tanks and vehicles are nowhere to be seen, replaced by horses, mules, camels and donkeys (Zech. 14:15).

The earth has been scorched by extreme heat and the lack of water has killed the foliage. Forest fires have devastated woodlands and structure. Starvation is constant and some resort to cannibalism. With enormous effort, the world's armies gather to fight as in millenniums past—face-to-face and hand to hand, they will either live or die.

With the formation of the military fully assembled on the morning prepared for the assault, the designated land will be filled with the massive army. A strange phenomenon will begin to form. As the morning sun begins to rise, it then faded, giving way to a very dull light. Bewilderment will grip each man as he stands in a twilight zone of neither day nor night (Zech. 14:6–7). Some soldiers began to imagine that they are under attack and the battle began.

The Israelite army will stand against the invading armies of the world. It will be a repeat of little David and the giant Goliath. The world against a tiny neighbor whose only wrong was that they exist. The beast's army soon captures Jerusalem. The homes are ransacked, the goods taken, the women raped, and half the people will be taken as captives (Zech. 14:2).

However, the Israelites will not be alone, and a strange light will have no logical explanation. What happens next is also without equal. The beast's soldiers, as they stand, the flesh on their feet will begin to rot, their eyes will dissolve in their sockets, and their tongues will rot in their mouths (Zech. 14:12).

Animals used against the Jews suddenly are smitten with panic, confusion, and blindness. Also, those who are riding on the creatures will lose their sanity (Zech. 12:4). The war that should be over instead intensifies. With insufficient light, soldiers mistakenly identify their own soldiers as the enemy. It had happened in other wars and now again. Each soldier in combat fights against his own comrade. "A great panic from the Lord will be among them. Everyone will seize the hand of his neighbor, and they will attack each other" (Zech. 14:13, 1 Samuel 14:15).

The Final Conquest

When things could not become worse, worse will come. Jesus had said that a sign of the end would be an increase of earthquakes. "It will be a time of distress unequaled in any period of earth's history. Unless those days had been cut short no life would survive" (Matt. 24). "There will be flashes of lightning, rumblings of thunder and a severe earthquake, such a mighty and great earthquake as had not occurred since men were on the earth" (Rev. 16:18). All the islands that existed in the seas disappeared, all the great mountains that stand on the earth will vanish. Huge hailstones, each weighing as much as a hundred pounds will fall from the sky on people. Jerusalem will split into three parts, and all the cities throughout the earth will be destroyed (Rev. 16:18–21, Ezekiel 38:18–23).

New York City will be flattened, and Chicago will cease to exist. All the cities of the world, whether small or great, will be no more. A thousand years prior to John, Isaiah saw a similar vision of the end of days. There will be violence even in the heavens. The sun will be darkened, and the heavens will shake. Eruptions within the earth will become so severe that the earth will literally move from its present orbit. The North Pole will no longer be north, and a cluster of new stars will rule the night. The death toll over the earth will be so drastic that to find a live human will be as rare as finding gold (Isa. 13:11–16).

The number of men who die in combat will be enormous. According to Isaiah, "In that day seven women shall take hold of one man saying, we will eat our own food and wear our own apparel; only let us be called by your name" (Isa. 4:1). The slaughter of soldiers will be massive at Armageddon. Two hundred miles of scattered bodies, some that have fallen on others who have also fallen to a height touching a horse's bridle. In five feet of blood and guts lay the world's great army and its leader, the beast (Rev. 14:20).

"I saw the beast, and the kings of the earth and their armies, gathered together to make war. And I saw an angel standing in the sun; he cried with a loud voice to all the fowls of heaven; come, gather yourselves together for supper. You may eat the flesh of kings, of captains, of mighty men" (Rev. 19:17–21, Ezekiel 38:39).

A Thousand Years of Peace

The war ended with few survivors. Cities have been turned into rubble, forests into burned out wastelands. Earth's water supplies have been contaminated, and the great oceans no longer exist (Rev. 21:1). Mountains have been reduced to hills (Matt. 16:20, Ezek. 38:20) and the earth has almost returned to its inherent beginning. Satellites, spacecraft, electronics, medication, food storage, and supplies have vanished. Without the technology or equipment to provide these products, man is reduced to his primitive state. God gave knowledge to man. When man reached his pinnacle, man dismissed God as deity, elevating himself as a god.

For seven months, the house of Israel will be burying the massive army (Ezek. 39:11–16). Each day will convince even the most agnostic Jew that this elimination of a complete powerful military had to be an act of God. The invading army was so massive that just the wood used in their weapons supplied Israel with sufficient fuel for the next seven years (Ezek. 39:9–10). When Jerusalem split into three parts, a spring of pure water gushed up from the earth that flowed, forming two rivers, one that flowed east and the other west (Zech. 14:8). This likely occurred elsewhere throughout the earth.

The oceans no longer exist, due to the fact that they were not a part of the original earth (Rev. 21:1). The seas that once existed were a result of God's judgment on earth in two separate occasions. The first world was sealed under a torrent of water that remained for an unknown duration of time until God moved upon the face of the waters (Gen. 1:2). The second devastation by water occurred in Noah's day after which God said that He would never again destroy the entire earth by water (Gen. 9:11).

A New Heaven and a New Earth

With a total devastation of the old earth, human life will begin as in a new world. Even our view of the heavens will have changed as a result of earth's shift, during its orbit (Isaiah 13:13). Despite that the woodlands have been ravaged by drought and heat, the seeds fallen in the earth are quick to respond to a proper climate. Without medication, human life will resume back to a natural state. The mother not leaving home because of many children, and a father who will work the field to provide food for his home. There will be peace on earth for exactly one thousand years. The climate will be perfect, the food and water will be fresh and nutritious. Life will be long and people healthy (Isa. 65:17–25). Not even the thought of war will not exist (Isa. 2:4). Within a thousand years, earth's population will have again filled the earth and Jerusalem will be the capital of the new world (Zech. 14:16–19, Isa. 2:2–4).

The Spirit World

In the final seven years, people's hatred for God will be constant. Standing before God were those who had been tortured and killed because of their obedience to God. People were martyred from every nation, tribe, and tongue, a multitude so massive that they could not be numbered (Rev. 7:9–14). Hate toward God caused the death of saints and prophets (Rev. 16:6). Many were beheaded because of their witness of Jesus (Rev. 20:4). "O Lord, how long must we suffer?" (Rev. 20:4).

Little Israel was confronted by an enormous giant. All of earth's nations have gathered to smite Israel with a final blow. In that moment of history, when all odds were against Israel, a miracle changed the entire world.

Jerusalem will be victimized by an overwhelming force. Without hope the devastated Israelites will be grasping for their last moments as the invasion force rummages through their city. Without hope and again without a home, they struggle to survive.

Suddenly from the sky came the appearance of one who filled the entire heavens. His eyes were as flaming fire, His sword was such that it could smite the nations, and He came to make war. He slaughtered the armies of the wicked and fed their flesh to the creatures of the world, but the beast and the false prophet He took alive and cast them into the lake of fire (Rev. 19:11–21).

The Bible states that when Christ returns to earth, "every eye shall see Him" (Rev. 1:7). He will not come alone; the armies of heaven follow Him (Rev. 19:14). The heavenly army consists of all who were redeemed from all past ages and those who have died just moments before Christ's arrival, including all the righteous who remain alive at Jesus's return. "The Lord Himself will descend from heaven with a shout, with the voice of an archangel, and with the trumpet of God. The dead in Christ will rise first, then we who are alive and remain shall be caught up together with them in the clouds to meet the Lord in the air. And, thus we shall always be with the Lord" (1 Thess. 4:15–17). "We shall not all sleep (die) but we all shall be changed – in a moment, in the twinkling of an eye" (1 Corinthians 15:51–52).

On Christ's return, He is followed by God's army, and Christ sets down on the outskirts of Jerusalem, on the Mount of Olives. As His feet touch the earth the momentum of His being caused Jerusalem to split into two sections, forming a large valley (Zech. 14:3–5). Christ's second coming will cause earth's most massive earthquake. The mountains will fall to the earth and earth's orbit will shift. The earth will be transfigured into a new existence as a new earth.

New Earth

"The Lord will be King over the entire earth" (Zech. 14:9). There will be only one God. Only one religion will exist throughout the entire earth. Not even the thought of war will exist. In every aspect of life there will be signs that read "Holiness to the Lord" (Zech. 14:20–21). All the nations of the world will be required to go each year to worship the Lord in Jerusalem. Nations that fail to do so will suffer drought and illness (Zech. 14:17–19).

God's Army

The Lord's army will be formed in the air just prior to His ascension on earth. It will consist of humans who evaluated obedience to God beyond their own comfort and safety. They were willing to die in exchange for a new body and an eternal home. The redeemed people become the priests of God (Rev. 20:6) servants of Christ (Rev. 19:5) and will rule and reign with Christ on the earth (Rev. 20:4–6).

When true Christian dies, they are instantly in the presence of the Lord (2 Cor. 5:6–8). This new body is neither male nor female (Mk. 2:25), yet we shall be known even as we were known (1 Cor. 13:12). The spirit world cannot be detected by the material world. Today, we are in the constant presence of angels, both good and evil angels of whom we remain ignorant as to their presence. We as saints will join Christ at the moment of His second coming in the sky. We then work with the angels or replace them as the unseen rulers over the earth with Christ as the head (Rev. 20:4). Our new bodies will be as real as our existence is today, yet the new bodies will be eternal, not subject to death. From the days of Adam, humans have suffered war and killings. The millennium will be a thousand years of unprecedented peace on earth (Isa. 65:17–25).

Revelations informs us:

> "Behold, I come like a thief. Blessed is he
> who stays awake." (Rev. 16:15)

The sneak thief who comes and leaves without being seen was not part of the equation. The oriental thief in Jesus's day came with a gang banded together causing death and destruction as they stole the goods. When people moved to a new location, they traveled in groups to avoid attack (Lk. 2:44). The disciples preached the gospel but carried swords for protection (Matt. 26:51). A man alone was leaving Jerusalem for Jericho. Without defense, he was robbed, including his clothes, and left for dead (Lk. 10:30).

The moral lesson taught is not to be asleep, be constantly alert, ready to protect oneself from evil. No one knows the day or hour when Jesus comes for us. Death is in most cases unexpected. If we only knew, we would have prepared.

The End of the Millennium

Throughout the entire thousand years, Lucifer, who is the devil, and his cohorts were sealed in a prison within the earth, named Hell. Peace could not have existed on earth with a loose devil inciting evil. He was confined to Hell with all his fallen angels, which are many. However, Hell is not a permanent location but is a temporary holding pen (Rev. 20:7). At the end of the millennium, he and his angels are loosed from their prison. Instantly, he begins doing what he enjoys most-raising havoc with humanity again.

Obviously, what required years previously to instigate would again require a period to corrupt a substantial number of people. Lucifer soon locates those who were unhappy with their obligation to worship in Jerusalem and the devil again ignites anger against the Jews. He assembles an army in number that equals the sand of the sea and surrounds Jerusalem. Fire falls from the sky wiping out for a final time Lucifer's plot to destroy God and His people.

The Lake of Fire

Hell had been the temporary prison created for the devil and his angels (Matt. 25:41). The everlasting fire will not remain in the earth but in a distant place unknown to humans as the "lake of fire" (Rev. 19:20, 20:10). It is in that world named "the lake of fire" that will last "forever and ever."

"It has been appointed for men once to die and then the judgment" (Heb. 9:27). The body dies turning back to dust. Yet we remain very much alive. In a nation governed by rules and law, when those laws are violated, the person may be held in a prison cell until the judge settles the dispute. The saints, when they die, go to a place called Paradise.

The sinner awaits trial in Hell (Lk. 23:43). No one dies in Hell (Mk. 9:44–48). Being a spirit, there is no physical body to burn, yet despite the lack of a body, no one enjoys Hell. The one voice we hear from hell had been a very selfish person while on earth. In Hell, he was very displeased with his plight (Lk. 16:19–31). The great judgment comes at the end of this final war. All who have died without salvation are retained in hell until they are proven innocent or guilty by the Judge of all mankind. "Then I saw a great white throne and Him who was seated on it. Earth and sky fled from His presence, and there was no escape for them. I saw the dead, great and small, standing before the throne, and books were opened. Another book was opened, which is the book of life. The dead were judged according to what they had done as recoded in the book. The sea gave up the dead that were in it, and death and Hades gave up the dead that were in them, and each person was judged according to what he had done. Then death and Hades were thrown into the lake of fire. The lake of fire is the second death. If anyone's name was not found written in the book of life, he was thrown into the lake of fire" (Rev. 20:11–15).

Jerusalem

The city of Jerusalem plays a major part in church history. It began when God told Abram to leave his family and country to a land that God would lead him to (Gen. 12). Because God had given the land to Abram who became Abraham, the site became contested by every alien stranger worldwide.

Israel became the home of the prophets, the birth and crucifixion of Christ, the home of every disciple, the site of Christ's return, and will be the center of worship during the millennium. Jerusalem is the pulpit God used to proclaim His message of salvation to the nations of the world. When God created a land in the heavens for His elect, He named it the "New Jerusalem."

A New Earth

On Satan's release from hell, he quickly begins his quest for world dominance and is promptly disposed of eternally in the lake of fire. It is a new world without a devil, the author of death and destruction. The earth does not evaporate, neither do the heavens vanish. Ecclesiastes 1:4 informs us that "the earth abides forever." Psalm 104:5 states, "God laid the foundations of the earth firmly, and it will never be moved." The prophet Zechariah states that Jerusalem will never again be destroyed" (Zech. 14:11). Life on earth will resume as it had from the beginning.

The New Jerusalem

The saints in their spiritual body had worked for Christ a thousand years on earth. Looking toward the sky, there appeared a sight difficult to describe. High above earth was a brilliant light unlike any other. In the light was an object with a soft glow, the glow as from a very precious stone, a jasper stone clear as crystal.

The old Jerusalem will always remain as the central location for humankind to find rest and salvation. Without salvation on earth, there can be no righteousness, and without holiness no man shall see the Lord (Heb. 12:14). Those with sin cannot enter the New Jerusalem. Rev. 21:27. Only those who obey God's commands may enter that city (Rev. 22:14). No human on earth will ever qualify to enter this city. The New Jerusalem is for the redeemed exclusively after the rapture. "I John saw the holy city, New Jerusalem, coming down from God out of heaven—God shall wipe away all tears from their eyes, there will be no more death no sorrow, no crying, nor pain. Those who are willing to overcome will inherit all things, I will be his God, and he will be my son. But "The cowardly, unbelieving, perverts, murderers, the immoral, those who practice magic, who worship idols, and all liars shall have their part in the lake which burns with fire and brimstone. This will be their second death" (Rev. 21).

The New Jerusalem is a brilliant city, its streets are pure gold. It has twelve gates, each is a single pearl. Its foundations or footings are garnished with the most rare and desired gems with walls of jasper. John goes on to describe the city's shape and size, naming the numerous gems contained in its structure. It has no similarity to the physical world and it is an object that remains in the sky high above earth. Without the need of a sun, its glow is constant.

The righteous have reigned with Christ throughout the millennium. As unseen agents, advising and protecting earthlings, directed by Christ for a thousand years. This should qualify any person for the tasks ahead. If indeed we have become Kings and priests, we likely will do more through eternity than look at each other and sing (Rev. 5:10). God is forever working. Each of the angels has obligations. At the end of the thousand years, our reign with Christ does not end. We permanently are appointed by God to be Kings and priests for a purpose. We are to rule and reign with Christ for ever and ever (Rev. 22:5).

It is interesting that in the New Jerusalem the gates never close. They will remain open always, which seems to indicate that its inhabitants are free to come and go at any time. Is it possible that we become the ministering spirits to those on earth? Many of us have always assumed that our heavenly home is in a land beyond the universe. We were wrong! The New Jerusalem will remain in this universe, in the sky, in the heavens, high above the earth and will remain our eternal home.

About the Author

Paul Ekroth
Reverend, teacher, pastor, evangelist, business executive.

Paul, is a descendant from Swedish speaking immigrants. In the early 19th century his mother's father, founded two Swedish speaking churches in Worcester Massachusetts. Paul's father had never entered a church until the age of 20. For the first time dad heard the message of salvation in his native language. At that time he received the message of salvation. Dad also met the pastor's daughter who became his wife.

Dad, taught me the values of hard work. Mother taught me how to pray and Bible values. Paul became a youth evangelist.

In 1956, Paul graduated after four years of training in the Chicago Bible College where he earned an advanced teachers certificate. On August 12, 1956 in a ceremony, Paul was ordained as a minister of the gospel.

CPSIA information can be obtained
at www.ICGtesting.com
Printed in the USA
BVHW03*0056240718
522426BV00004B/54/P

9 781642 589665